EDUCATION LIBRARY
MCF - STILLWATER

T0111751

NORTH KOREA

MAJOR WORLD NATIONS

NORTH KOREA

Amy K. Nash

CHELSEA HOUSE PUBLISHERS
Philadelphia

Chelsea House Publishers

Contributing Author: James Rhoderick

Copyright © 1999 by Chelsea House Publishers,
a division of Main Line Book Co.
All rights reserved.
Printed and bound in the United States of America.

3   5   7   9   8   6   4   2

Library of Congress Cataloging-in-Publication Data

Nash, Amy K.
North Korea / Amy K. Nash.
p.   cm. — (Major world nations)
Reprint. Originally published: 1991. (Places and peoples
of the world).
Includes index.
Summary: Examines the geography, history, government, society,
economy, and transportation of North Korea.
ISBN 0–7910–4746–6 (hc)
1. Korea (North)—Juvenile literature.   [1. Korea (North)]
I. Title.   II. Series.
DS932.N34   1997
951.93—dc21   97–21857
CIP

CONTENTS

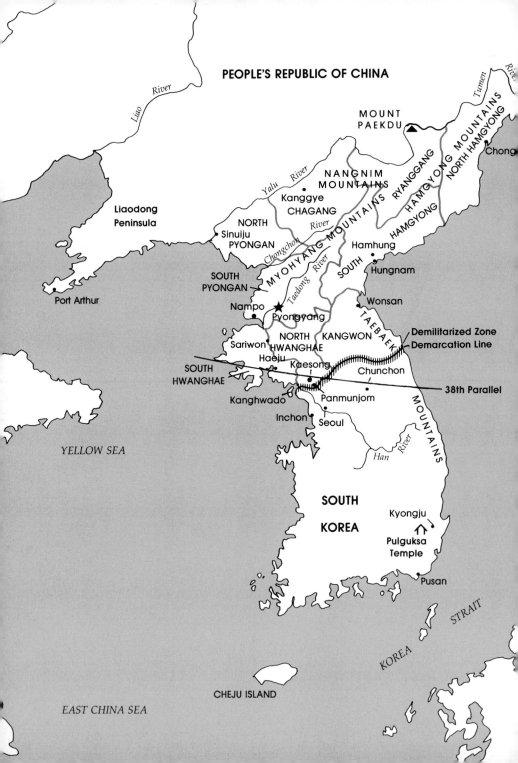

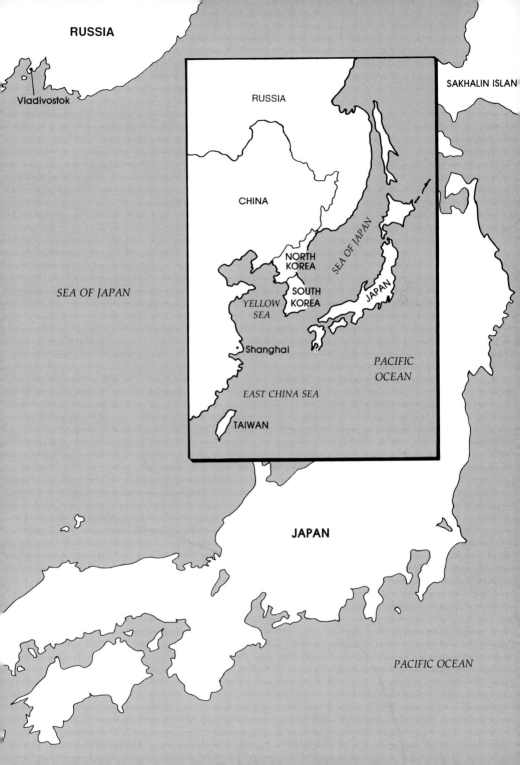

FACTS AT A GLANCE

Land and People

Official Name of Country	Democratic People's Republic of Korea (North Korea)
Area	46,540 square miles (120,538 square kilometers)
Highest Point	Mount Paekdu, 9,003 feet (2,744 meters)
Capital	Pyongyang (population 2.6 million)
Major Cities	Hamhung (population 790,000), Chongjin (population 760,000), Nampo (population 700,000), Kaesong (population 350,000), Wonsan (population 355,000)
Major Rivers	Yalu, Tumen, Taedong
Major Mountain Ranges	Taebaek, Nangnim
Population	24 million
Population Density	514 people per square mile (198 per square kilometer)
Population Distribution	Urban, 70 percent; rural, 30 percent

Language	Korean
Ethnic Groups	Korean, 100 percent
Literacy Rate	99 percent
Religions	Buddhism, shamanism, Chundo Kyo, Christianity
Average Life Expectancy	Male, 67 years; female 73 years

Economy

Natural Resources	Iron ore, copper, lead, zinc, manganese, coal
Major Products	Rolled steel, ships, chemical fertilizers, cement
Major Crops	Rice, corn, coarse grains, potatoes, vegetables, soybeans
Chief Imports	Machinery, petroleum, coking coal, wheat
Chief Exports	Semimanufactured metal products, magnesite powder, lead, cement
Energy Sources	Coal and hydroelectric power
Employment of Work Force	Agriculture, 36 percent; industry and services, 64 percent
Average Per Capita Income	1,850 won in 1995 (U.S. $920)
Major Trading Partners	Russia, China, Japan, and Germany
Currency	Won

Government

Form of Government	Communist state, one-leader rule
Political Party	Korean Workers' party
Head of State	President of state and secretary-general of Korean Workers' party

Legislative Branch	Supreme People's Assembly, consisting of 655 elected officials
Cabinet	Central People's Committee, headed by the president of state
Municipal Administration	9 provinces, 4 cities
Eligibility to Vote	North Korean citizens at least 17 years of age can vote in the Supreme People's Assembly elections, held approximately every four years

HISTORY AT A GLANCE

8000–3000 B.C. Tungusic tribes migrate to the Korean peninsula from the northern regions of central Asia.

900–800 B.C. Inhabitants of the peninsula use bronze tools
for the first time.

300 B.C. China recognizes the walled-town state of Old
Choson (present-day Pyongyang).

109 B.C.–A.D. 53 Chinese Han dynasty military forces turn Old
Choson into the Chinese-controlled territory of
Lo-lang.

53–668 Korean history is first recorded (in Chinese)
during the Period of the Three Kingdoms. The
three states of Koguryo, Paekche, and Silla
develop independently into important cultural
centers and fight among themselves for control
over the peninsula. Buddhism and Confucianism reach the peninsula.

668 With the support of the Chinese Tang dynasty,
Silla troops defeat the Koguryo army and
unify all of Korea under Silla rule.

936 After defeating the rebel leader Kyonhwon,
who had invaded Silla's capital, General Wang

Kon unites the peninsula under Koryo rule.
The Koryo dynasty reigns until the end of the
14th century.

1231 Mongol troops invade Koryo.

1234 Movable cast metal type is invented in Korea.

1274–81 Kublai Khan, the Mongol emperor of China,
enlists thousands of Korean men and ships to
invade Japan. Typhoons destroy the fleets.

1392 General Yi Song-gye seizes the capital of
Koryo and declares himself king. The Yi dynasty rules until the beginning of the 20th century.

15th century Yi scholars invent the Korean alphabet, *hangul*,
which is still in use today.

1592 Toyotomi Hideyoshi, the military governor of
Japan, invades Korea. Korean Admiral Yi Sun-
sin and his "turtle ships" retaliate, and by
1598, Japanese forces retreat, leaving Korea
devastated by the war.

17th century Christian missionaries first reach the peninsula.

1785 The Korean government bans all forms of
Western learning.

1873 Confucian officials drive Taewon-gun, the last
powerful leader of the Yi dynasty, from the
throne. Japan forces Korea to sign a treaty
opening three of its ports for trade with Japan.

1894–95 Leaders of the Tonghak sect instigate peasant
revolts throughout the country. Japan declares
war on China and is victorious.

1895–1904 Japanese forces attack Russian forces at Port
Arthur, beginning the Russo-Japanese War.
Japan wins the war.

September 1905 Russia and Japan sign the Treaty of
Portsmouth. Korea becomes Japan's protectorate.

August 29, 1910	Japan annexes Korea, making it a Japanese colony until the end of World War II.
February 1945	The United States and the Soviet Union agree at the Yalta Conference that after Japan surrenders to the Allies, the Soviet Union will become the trustee of the part of Korea north of the 38th Parallel and the United States will become the trustee of the portion south of that line.
August 15, 1945	Japan surrenders, ending World War II. Koreans celebrate their independence in the streets. But Soviet and U.S. forces soon occupy their designated portions of the peninsula.
August 15, 1948	The Republic of Korea (South Korea) is proclaimed with Syngman Rhee as president.
September 9, 1948	The Democratic People's Republic of Korea is established with Kim Il Sung as premier.
June 25, 1950	North Korean troops launch a surprise attack across the 38th Parallel and eventually take Seoul. The Korean War begins.
June 28, 1950	The UN Command forces, under U.S. general Douglas MacArthur, come to South Korea's aid.
November 1950	Chinese troops come to North Korea's aid.
July 27, 1953	Military leaders from North Korea, the Chinese People's Volunteers, and the UN Command sign an armistice ending the Korean War. A cease-fire line is drawn along the 38th Parallel, and the demilitarized zone is created.
October 5, 1966	Kim Il Sung gives a speech at a party conference that establishes North Korea's political independence from all other Communist nations.
August 1971	The two Koreas allow their Red Cross societies to hold talks for reuniting the Korean families

separated since the end of the Korean War.
No progress is made.

September 1985 The two Red Cross societies arrange for a
series of brief reunions in Seoul and
Pyongyang for 100 members of the
separated families.

January 1988 Kim Il Sung declares that the two Koreas
should recognize one another.

September 1990 The North and South Korean prime ministers
finish two unprecedented days of talks in
Seoul.

December 1991 Signed declaration forbids both sides to build
or test nuclear weapons.

March 1993 Tensions rise as North Korea withdraws
from the Nuclear Non-Proliferation Treaty.
Talks resume later.

July 1994 Kim Il Sung dies. His son takes power.

Summer 1995 Record floods force the government to ask
the world for humanitarian aid.

April 1996 North Korea denies its armistice obligation
and sends troops briefly into the demilita-
rized zone.

March 1997 A high-ranking North Korean official defects
to Seoul and warns of severe famine and military desperation in the North.

NORTH KOREA

Even though he died in 1994, Kim Il Sung is still revered throughout North Korea as the Great Leader. His legacy lives on through his son, Kim Jong Il, who succeeded him as North Korea's leader, although some observers question whether the son has the same political ability as the father.

1

North Korea and the World

Known to its people as *Choson* (Land of Morning Calm), Korea occupies a mountainous peninsula in northeastern Asia. It stretches southward from Manchuria (northeastern China) and Russian Siberia for close to 600 miles (966 kilometers) down to the Korea Strait. Korea is separated from China on the west by the Yellow Sea and from Japan on the east by the Sea of Japan. Western societies have traditionally viewed the Korean peninsula as a remote region of the world. They have often referred to it as the Hermit Kingdom because it remained isolated from the West until the 19th century. Yet it actually holds a central position on the globe, neighboring three major world powers—Russia, China, and Japan.

For centuries Korea served as a bridge across which Chinese culture made its way to Japan. Situated on a peninsula, it has had easy access to these other cultures and has suffered countless invasions by its neighbors. It is no wonder that the Korean people have found it necessary to fiercely defend their identity as a separate culture. Taking a closer look, it is also apparent that the Land of Morning Calm has not always been so peaceful.

Since the end of World War II in 1945, an artificial barrier along the 38th Parallel (a line of latitude on the globe) has divided the peninsula into two distinct countries—North Korea (officially called the Democratic People's Republic of Korea) and South Korea (formally known as the Republic of Korea). When Japan unconditionally surrendered to the Allies on August 15, 1945, bringing an end to World War II, Korea gained its freedom from Japan, which had occupied the peninsula since 1905.

On the same day, the victorious Allied leaders, U.S. president Harry S. Truman and Soviet leader Joseph Stalin, signed an agreement that designated temporary occupation zones on the peninsula. This agreement stated that the United States would

Portraits of Kim Il Sung (center) and two Soviet leaders, Lenin (left) and Joseph Stalin (right), adorn a public building in North Korea in 1947. The Soviet Union acted as a trustee of North Korea until 1948, when North Korea declared itself an independent Communist state.

serve as an international trustee for all of Korea south of the 38th Parallel (including Seoul, Korea's largest city) and the Soviet Union would act as trustee for the northern half of the peninsula. This temporary measure became a permanent division in 1948, when North Korea formally declared itself an independent sovereign state under a Communist system of government and South Korea became an anti-Communist republican regime. (In theory, communism is a form of government under which all property is owned by the state and all goods are distributed equally among the people. Communism, in its ideal form, has never been fully achieved by any country, although many have tried.)

Because leaders of both North Korea and South Korea sought control over the entire peninsula, for three years (1950–53) a devastatingly self-destructive war ensued, ending in a stalemate with an even more rigidly defined boundary created to bisect the land. This boundary, called a demilitarized zone (DMZ), extends just over a mile (2,000 meters) on both sides of a military demarcation line and covers a total of 487 square miles (1,261 square kilometers) of neutral territory. More than 1 million military troops eye one another from both sides of the barbed wire and mine fields that define the DMZ.

Although South Korea has opened its doors wide to international trade and has experienced what experts call an economic miracle since the end of the Korean War—when the country was virtually destroyed—North Korea has lagged behind. Most Americans know South Korea for its advanced electronics and the Hyundai Excel—which, when first introduced in 1986, became the most successful new car import in U.S. automotive history. They recognize the name of South Korea's capital, Seoul, as the site of the 1988 Olympic Games. But what does the average American, or any citizen in the West, really know about North Korea? What does the name Pyongyang mean to most Westerners? South Korea may have shaken off the Hermit Kingdom label, but what about its northern neighbor?

The economy of North Korea grew very rapidly in the 1950s but has slowed since then. Its economy, based on heavy industry, actually began to shrink in the years after the Cold War ended, when it lost trade partners in Communist Eastern Europe and Russia. South Korea, on the other hand, has had the active economic and military support of the United States and Japan and now even has trade and political relations with China. North Korea has developed some trade with the south and other countries, but has poor credit for loans. Floods and energy shortages have further crippled the country's ability to feed itself and develop its industries. The government hopes to maintain control, but many feel that its inefficient and rigid regime, still spending heavily on the military, cannot survive without allies. The economy is in total decline, and the people face famine. North Korea must choose either to open up to more relations with the world—and risk change—or face dire economic consequences.

On September 5, 1990, South Korean delegates (left) shake hands with their North Korean counterparts prior to the first round of talks in Seoul. The dialogue, which was the first high-level meeting since the two Koreas were divided in 1945, included discussions of such issues as reunification and joint business ventures.

Perhaps even more important than the economic issue is the ongoing question of whether reunification will occur. The people of North and South Korea share one language, one history, and one cultural base that goes back at least 5,000 years. On the minds of all Koreans, whatever their political leanings may be and wherever they may live, is the issue of reunifying the two countries into one. Ten million Koreans remain separated from family members because of the division at the 38th Parallel. Since the end of the Korean War, citizens from both the north and the south have made efforts at reunification and have failed. With the North Korean economic and political situation offering so many uncertainties, the prospects for reunification in the near future are impossible to predict.

The ranges around Mount Paekdu stretch along the northern border of Ryanggang province. Almost 80 percent of Korea is mountainous.

2

A Land of High Mountains and Sparkling Streams

Roughly the size of the state of Mississippi, North Korea constitutes almost 55 percent of the peninsula's total land area. Approximately 46,540 square miles (120,538 square kilometers) of the peninsula's entire area of 85,052 square miles (220,283 square kilometers) are located above the 38th Parallel. About 3,000 islands, most of which are located near the southern coast, lie off of Korea's estimated 10,725 miles (17,300 kilometers) of coastline. The name "Korea" derives from the Koryo dynasty that ruled the peninsula from the 10th to 14th centuries. (The word *dynasty* refers to the succession of rulers from one particular family and to the period during which the family ruled.) The term *Korea*, which many believe Marco Polo (the 13th-century Venetian explorer) took with him to Europe, means "land of high mountains and sparkling streams." It is especially accurate in describing the North Korean terrain, which is 80 percent mountain ranges and uplands.

Forests cover approximately four-fifths of Korea. More than 100 species of trees grow in North Korea, including spruce, fir, maple, oak, apple, and jujube.

Korea's geography has greatly influenced its history. Only one-fifth of the land is cultivated; forests cover the other four-fifths. Surrounded by water on three sides, the peninsula has, in many ways, isolated its inhabitants from the rest of the world. But because Korea shares the bulk of its northern border with Manchuria (except for the 11-mile stretch of the Tumen River that separates the northeastern corner of North Korea from Russian Siberia, below Vladivostok), Chinese colonists discovered an accessible route into the peninsula. Ancient tribes from the Manchurian plains easily crossed the Yalu (Amnok-kang) and Tumen (Tuman-gang) rivers, which serve as the present-day northern border between North Korea and China. They crossed the frozen rivers on foot or on horseback in the winter and built ships to cross the thawed waters in the summer.

The geographic differences between the northern and southern portions of the peninsula accentuate the political division between the two Koreas. With its milder climate and extensive, fertile plains, South Korea has a population more than double that of North Korea, even though North Korea occupies more land area. Harsher winters, shorter growing seasons, and a rugged terrain mean a more arduous way of life for those dwelling in the northern area of the peninsula.

Mountains and Rivers

Two major Korean mountain ranges—the Taebaek and the Nangnim—run parallel to one another in a north-to-south direc-

A waterfall cascades down the slope of Mount Myohyang, northeast of Pyongyang. Sweet-smelling junipers abound on the mountain and are responsible for giving Myohyang its name, which means "singular and fragant." Myohyang's captivating scenery includes numerous cliffs, streams, and fantastic rocks.

tion. For centuries these mountains prevented any kind of communication between the eastern and western sections of the peninsula. Smaller systems of mountains that originate in the two larger ranges run parallel to one another in a northeast-to-southwest direction. In North Korea, these ranges include the Kangnam, Chogyu, Myohyang, Myorak, and Hamgyong mountains.

Most of the largest rivers in Korea flow westward from the Taebaek Mountains that line the east coast. The great Yalu and Tumen rivers both originate on the slopes of Mount Paekdu ("Mount of Eternal Snow"), which rises 9,003 feet (2,744 meters) above sea level, the highest elevation in all of Korea. The Yalu River flows southwestward into the Yellow Sea and has a channel length of 490 miles (790 kilometers). The Tumen River flows in a northeasterly direction, emptying into the Sea of Japan, and has a channel length of 323 miles (521 kilometers).

North Korea also has a large number of smaller rivers and streams. Located on the southern bank of one of these smaller rivers, the Chongchon, is Tongnyonggul, Korea's most famous cave. It is about 3 miles (5 kilometers) long, and several of its chambers measure close to a tenth of a mile (150 meters) wide and 55 yards (50 meters) high. Within its walls are stalagmites, stalactites, ponds, and streams. During the summer, the rivers swell with the rainfall that accompanies the persistently changing winds known as monsoons, causing floods in the valley plains. During the rest of the year, the dry climate causes the rivers to reach dangerously low water levels, often exposing the riverbeds.

The rivers have greatly influenced the historical development of Korea. Capital cities such as Seoul, Pyongyang, and Puyo developed as port cities alongside major rivers. Pyongyang, the present-day capital of North Korea, is located on the banks of the Taedong River. With the introduction of the railroad (and, eventually, automobiles), the rivers became a less important form of transportation. Today, Koreans use their vast network of rivers for irrigating rice fields and for generating hydroelectricity.

Three Geographic Regions of North Korea

Three distinct geographic regions make up the land area occupied by North Korea. A mountainous, cold, forbidding land, the northern interior has for centuries isolated Koreans from adjoining areas of the Asian mainland. The Yalu and Tumen rivers and their tributaries flow in deep, narrow valleys within the region. Once

Loggers work amid the snow-covered trees of Mount Rangrin. North Korea has harsher winters than South Korea, and its craggy terrain often means a more formidable way of life for those who reside there.

volcanic and now snow-covered most of the year, Mount Paekdu is located in the northern end of this region. Lava flows, which came from the mountain, cover the surrounding area, creating a plateaulike terrain. A large crater lake called Chonji, which means "heavenly lake," is located at its summit. Mountain ridges rise abruptly between river valleys in the region, making travel very treacherous. To the southeast, a sharp drop spills into the coastal region along the Sea of Japan. To the southwest, a more gradual descent leads to the hills and mountains of the northwestern region. The spruce, fir, and larch forests that cover the mountain slopes constitute an important base for the forest industry in the country. Similarly, the swift-flowing streams provide hydroelectric power.

The northeastern region extends along the coast of the Sea of Japan. Rivers flowing from the northern interior highland carve out valleys along the coast. Between the valleys, hills and mountains extend out into the sea. The Tumen Valley, which runs along the northern border with eastern Russia, serves as a passageway from ports along the Sea of Japan to Manchuria. The cold Liman Current forces later summer seasons and occasional fogs that lead to crop failures. Water from the slopes and cliffs produce

The dam of the Supung Power Station on the Yalu (Amnok-kang) River helps provide North Korea with its supply of hydroelectricity. The image of a hydroelectric power station is part of the design of North Korea's national emblem.

hydroelectric power for the industries developing along the coast. The country's major ports — Chongjin, Hungnam, and Wonsan— also line the eastern coast.

The northwestern region is the most densely populated area in North Korea. Pyongyang is located in the heart of the area, and other important cities and ports in the region include Sinuiju, Kaesong, and Nampo. As an important entryway for ancient tribes migrating from the north, the northwestern region has been home to civilizations for thousands of years. Large alluvial plains (made of sand and clay deposits) surround the mouths of the Yalu and Taedong rivers, as well as those of other rivers that drain the region, and pine forests blanket the mountainous sections. Plains and low hills fill the Hwanghae peninsula, which stretches out into the Yellow Sea.

Climate

The diverse terrain of the country is reflected in the climate, which is influenced by the air masses of the Asian continent, especially

Pyongyang, the capital of North Korea, has a population of 2.6 million.

those of Siberia. The northern interior experiences long, bitterly cold winters—with average temperatures well below freezing—that last approximately five months of the year, during which time most of the rivers are completely frozen. January temperatures average around -6° Fahrenheit (-27° Celsius), whereas summer temperatures in the valleys average around 60° F (16° C), with lower temperatures in the mountains. Spring (April and May) and autumn (October and November) each last only about two months.

The yearly rainfall ranges from 30 to 40 inches (750 to 1,000 millimeters), and 60 percent of it occurs in the summer (June through September). This profuse amount of summer rain makes the land highly suited to rice farming.

The cooling effects of the Liman Current, which flows southward through the Sea of Japan, produces the northeast coastal area's relatively cool summers. Although the winters are cold, they are not as extreme as those in the northern interior. January temperatures average 15° F (-10° C) in the north, 21° F (-5° C) in the central coastal area, and 25° F (-3° C) in the south. Heavy rainfall covers the region, especially in the mountainous area close to the sea, and in some years the annual rainfall exceeds 50 inches (1,300 millimeters). The northwestern plains and hills also experience severely cold winters, but extremely hot, wet summers counterbalance them. More than half of the annual rainfall, which averages 37 inches (940 millimeters) in Pyongyang, occurs in July and August. Winters are colder in the north and slightly warmer along the western coast.

Plant and Animal Life

Vegetation in North Korea resembles that of Manchuria. Cold-temperate plants such as evergreens grow in abundance in the northern mountain areas. Great forests of spruce, fir, birch, and larch envelop the northern interior. Hardwood trees—maple, basswood, poplar, oak, ash, hornbeam, elm, chestnut, hackberry, and even some magnolia and Japanese yew—thrive in the central and southern portions of the country. Apple trees, such as the Pukchong and Hwangju (named for the places where they are grown), prosper in South Hamgyong and North Hwanghae provinces, where pears, persimmon, jujube, peach, apricot, cherry, and plum trees are also commonly grown. Herbal plants—many of which are used for medicinal purposes, such as Korean rhubarb (aids digestion), pullocho, or elixir mushroom (aids low blood pressure), the root of the white broad bellflower (relieves coughing), and the ginseng root (a cure-all)—are also scattered throughout the country. Until the 19th century, forests covered most of the peninsula, but insect blights and wood-hungry farmers eventually left many of the hills and mountain slopes bare. North Korea has made a successful effort in recent years to reforest the land.

The diverse array of animal life found in North Korea is similar to that of Europe. Many of the species are also the same as, or closely related to, those found in parts of Manchuria and Siberia. They include deer, roe deer, Amur goral (a type of antelope), Manchurian weasel, brown bear, Siberian tiger, lynx, northern pika (a small mammal that resembles a rabbit), water shrew (a tiny mouselike mammal), striped hamster, muskrat, Manchurian ring-necked pheasant, black grouse, hawk owl, three-toed woodpecker, and countless others.

A remarkable game sanctuary has developed within the DMZ. Because of an unspoken agreement between the opposing troops along the barbed-wire barrier, migrating birds (especially an endangered species of Siberian crane) flock to the area undisturbed. Other wildlife also have found a peaceful home within the mine fields of the most volatile spot on the peninsula.

The main statue of Buddha in Sokkuram Grotto, a secluded temple in a cave, was carved in the 8th century during the unified Silla period. The Buddha, sitting cross-legged, measures about 10 feet (3 meters) tall and is considered by many to be one of the period's sculptural masterpieces.

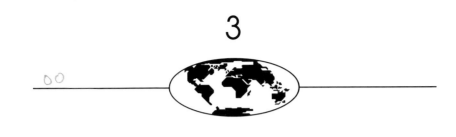

3

The Hermit Kingdom

The history of the independent socialist state of North Korea spans little more than 5 decades, yet archaeologists, specialists who study the life and culture of ancient peoples by excavating ancient cities and relics (axes and knives, for example), have found evidence that the peninsula was inhabited during the Paleolithic period (early Stone Age) as long as 40,000 to 50,000 years ago. Fossil remains (at such sites as Komunmoru Cave in Sangwon, Chommal Cave in Pojon-ni, and a dwelling site in Sokchang-hi) indicate that human beings lived in caves and on level ground, gathered fruit and berries, and hunted and fished in locations scattered throughout the peninsula during that time. There is no proof, however, that these inhabitants are the ethnic ancestors of today's Koreans.

The Korean people are believed to be the ethnic descendants of the Tungusic tribes (from the Altai mountain region in central Asia) that made the peninsula their home during the Neolithic period (later Stone Age), around 4000 B.C. Initially these migrating tribes built dwellings near the seashore and on the riverbanks.

They developed primitive religious and cultural practices that are reflected in their art. For example, the East Asian religion of shamanism, based on a belief in good and evil spirits that can only be appeased by priests or medicine men called shamans, reached the peninsula during this period. Shamanistic practices included the use of pottery with geometric designs that symbolized religious ideas and dances such as the *muchon*, which was performed as part of a ceremony to worship the heavens. They also had rituals for burying the dead and worshiped elements of the natural world—including mountains, trees, rivers, and especially the sun—as gods.

Agriculture arrived in the northern half of the peninsula around 3000 B.C. The first use of bronze tools in the north occurred around 900–800 B.C., but the Bronze Age did not make its way to southern Korea until 600 B.C. Cultural developments also reached northern Korea first. Korean Bronze Age dwellers lived in the mountains and relied on agriculture for food, adopting the Chinese method of rice cultivation, but they also hunted and fished.

The inhabitants during this period established walled-town states throughout the peninsula, and were ruled by Bronze Age chieftains. By the 4th century B.C., the end of the Bronze Age, several of these states were large enough to be recognized by China. They included Puyo in the Sungari River basin in the north, Yemaek along the middle portion of the Yalu River, Imdun in the Hamhung plain on the northeast seacoast, Chin just south of the Han River, and the most advanced of them all—Old Choson, located in the basin of the Liao and Taedong rivers, where Pyongyang is situated today.

Old Choson

The emergence of Old Choson coincided with the Period of War-ring States (403–221 B.C.) in China; therefore, it was able to expand independently while China endured many years of political turbulence. When China began to right itself politically, first during the Chin dynasty (249–207 B.C.) and then during the Han dynasty (200 B.C.–A.D. 220), Old Choson suffered the consequences. Revolts in China led to the flight of Chinese refugees into Old Choson. One of these refugees, Wiman, brought 1,000 other dissatisfied Chinese with him to drive King Chun from the throne and create a state called Wiman Choson in 190 B.C. This regime, however, lasted a mere 80 years, an unusually brief reign for a Korean dynasty. In 109 B.C., Emperor Han Wu Ti (called the Martial Emperor) of the Han dynasty attacked and conquered Wiman Choson, turning it into the Chinese-controlled territory of Lo-lang (Nangnang in Korean).

China had a pronounced influence on Korean culture during the Han dynasty. The system of laws expanded drastically in what had once been Old Choson. This development occurred partially because of the high incidence of theft by the Chinese merchants in Lo-lang. Old Choson society did not have as strong a sense of personal property as the Chinese did; therefore, the Chinese merchants easily took advantage of the local inhabitants. Neighboring societies did manage to maintain political independence from China while adopting various aspects of its culture. This situation would prove invaluable to Korea's future as an independently developed country.

The Three Kingdoms

Historians commonly refer to the first period of recorded Korean history (53 B.C.–A.D. 668) as the Period of the Three Kingdoms. The Three Kingdoms—Koguryo, Paekche, and Silla—were founded by members of the same ethnic group but during different periods and in distinct areas. The Three Kingdoms eventually competed with each other for supreme power, frequently changing alliances with one another and engaging in warfare. Located in the north-

A scene from one of the wall paintings in the burial chamber of the Tomb of Dancers (Koguryo dynasty, late 5th century) depicts a hunting scene. Mountains have been stylized in the form of wavy strips, whereas the hunters and animals have been represented realistically.

eastern region of the peninsula, Koguryo was the first, and largest, of these confederated states to develop. Legend has it that in 37 B.C., Chumong (the son of Yuhwa, who gave birth to him after being impregnated by the sun's rays) and others from Puyo settled in the center of the Yalu and Tung-chin river basins. Historical records more accurately reveal that by the 4th century B.C. Yemaek tribes inhabited the region, expanding to a population of 280,000 by the 2nd century B.C.

Lo-lang stood at the center of this state, and over the course of 400 years it grew into a great cultural center boasting Chinese art, philosophy, industry, and commerce. Because of its continual struggles with the Chinese, Koguryo maintained a strong military. Although Koguryo became an independent, centralized state in A.D. 53 with the fall of the Han dynasty (A.D. 220), it continued to endure attacks from outside Chinese forces.

As time passed, the state became more centralized. Five provinces evolved out of the earlier tribal regions, and the succession of the throne changed from a brother-to-brother pattern to one of father-to-son. In 313, under the direction of King Michon, the state seized power from the Chinese in yet another bloody battle. This finally put an end to four centuries of Chinese domination in the region, and the state rose to prominence as the most powerful state in northeast Asia.

King Kwanggaeto (whose name has been translated to mean both "Wide Open Land" and "Expander of Territory") earned a reputation as Koguryo's most famous ruler. During his reign (391–412), he conquered 65 walled towns, 1,400 villages, and aided the state of Silla, located in the southeastern portion of Korea, against Japanese invasion. (A monument to him still stands in southern Manchuria.)

Changsu, another noteworthy king of Koguryo, became known as "the long-lived" because he spent 78 years on the throne (413–491). Koguryo reached its height of glory during this time, and in 427, Changsu moved the capital from Kungnae-song (on what is now the Manchurian side of the Yalu River) to Pyongyang. This relocation made Koguryo more of a threat to the other developing states in Korea, particularly the kingdoms of Silla and Paekche.

Paekche evolved out of one of the walled-town states in the southwestern portion of the peninsula in the middle of the 3rd century A.D. By 246, it had enough military power to launch a counterattack against Lo-lang and Tai-fang forces (both controlled by the Chinese Wei dynasty) that had invaded the Han River region. In fact, the governor of Tai-fang was killed in this battle. King Koi ruled the region from around 234 to 286. He is believed to be the same person as King Kui, whom Paekche citizens later designated as their founder-king, honoring his memory with cere-monies four times a year.

During King Kun Chogo's reign (346–375), Paekche became a centralized aristocratic state, destroying the smaller neighboring states in the south. In 371, Paekche forces invaded Koguryo as far north as Pyongyang, killing Koguryo's King Kogugwon in the process. It also adopted the father-to-son pattern of succession and became a powerful force on the peninsula.

Silla developed from the walled-town state of Saro in south-eastern Korea sometime around A.D. 57–80. By the time of King Naemul's reign (356–402), it was recognized as a confederated kingdom. Around this time, Koguryo forces aided Silla in resisting attacks by Kaya (a small independent state located in the south between Paekche and Silla) and Japanese forces—attacks that had been initiated by Paekche forces. Father-to-son succession of the throne had been adopted by the time of King Nulchi's reign (418–458). Less than 100 years after Koguryo defended Naemul's throne against Paekche forces, Silla and Paekche had formed an alliance to resist advances by Koguryo.

Located on the Naktong River in the south-central part of the peninsula, Kaya had strong ties to tribes from both China and Japan but found itself caught between the powers of Silla and Paekche. Eventually it fell into the hands of the Silla kingdom in 562.

Koguryo, Paekche, and Silla each placed a strong emphasis on the thought of K'ung-Fu-tzu (called Confucius by Westerners), a Chinese scholar and philosopher who lived from 551 to 479 B.C. Through a code of morals and conduct, K'ung-Fu-tzu emphasized the importance of order, patience, moderation, service to the state, obedience, and devotion to one's elders. Koguryo established a National Confucian Academy (*Taehak*) as early as 372, the same year in which Buddhism, a religion based on the teachings of the ancient Indian philosopher Siddhārtha Gautama (known as Buddha), also reached Koguryo. Buddha (circa 563–483 B.C.) taught others that suffering in life is inherent and that one can be freed from it by mental and moral self-purification. Most historians believe that the monk Sundo brought images of Buddha and Buddhist sermons, called sutras, with him to Koguryo from north-eastern China. The monk Malananda brought Buddhism to Paekche 12 years later from the Yangtze River valley in central China.

The royal houses of Koguryo and Paekche readily accepted the religion, but when the monk Ado introduced Buddhist rituals to the outskirts of Silla during the 5th century, the inhabitants rejected the religion. King Pophung (514–540) wanted very much to declare Buddhism the state religion, but conservative aristocrats would not allow it. The story goes that in about 535 a young Buddhist in Pophung's court, named Ichadon, offered to sacrifice his life and become what is commonly referred to as a martyr in order to promote the religion to the aristocracy.

King Pophung and Ichadon devised a plan to give the appearance that Ichadon had built a Buddhist temple without royal consent, which meant that he would have to be executed. Before the execution, Ichadon predicted two miracles that would convince the aristocracy to believe in Buddhism: first, that his blood would be white as milk and, second, that his decapitated head would soar to a nearby hilltop. According to legend, these two events did occur, and the stunned aristocracy immediately accepted Buddhism as the state religion.

Soon thereafter, King Pophung supposedly relinquished the throne to become a monk, and his wife likewise retired to a nunnery. Every year on the fifth day of the eighth lunar month, the people of Silla commemorated the martyrdom of Ichadon. In all three of the kingdoms, Buddhism became the state religion only after the royal houses had accepted it.

For more than 250 years, the Three Kingdoms competed with one another for control over the whole peninsula. By the middle of the 7th century, disputes over the territorial rights of the Han River basin tore apart the Silla-Paekche alliance, and soon thereafter Silla joined forces with China's Tang dynasty. Together, Tang forces led by Su Ting-fang and Silla forces led by Kim Yu-sin attacked the Paekche capital of Sabi and destroyed the Paekche kingdom in 660. After eight bloody famine-stricken years,

Koguryo also fell to the combined forces of the Silla and Tang armies.

The Chinese hoped to take over the entire peninsula. Tang officials set up new regional divisions to govern both the conquered lands and Silla as well. Silla retaliated and captured Sabi in 671, taking Paekche away from the Chinese. Silla battled against Tang forces for another five years before it achieved its goal of controlling the entire peninsula. This great historical moment marked the true beginning of the independent development of Korean culture.

Unified Silla

Both the location of Silla and its native societal structures and customs help explain why it succeeded in the struggle among the Three Kingdoms to rule the peninsula. Because it took longer for Chinese culture to reach Silla's isolated region, changes could slowly be incorporated into the culture. Well-developed societal structures also protected it from invasion.

The *hwarang* ("flower of youth") corps fought Silla's battles and also functioned as elite training schools for future leaders. A strong religious element accompanied these voluntary youth organizations. They adopted the ways of Buddhism, making pilgrimages to sacred mountains and rivers to help them grasp the significance of nature, praying for peace and prosperity, and writing poems and music.

In the 7th century, Wongwang, a leading monk, not only devised new Buddhist rituals, he also reorganized the hwarang troops. At the request of two youths who wished to learn how to follow the teachings of Buddha, Wongwang created the *sesok ogye* (Five Principles for Secular Life), also known as the *Hwarang-do* (Law of the Hwarang). The Five Principles for Secular Life were as follows: (1) loyalty to the king, (2) devotion to one's parents, (3) loyalty to one's friends, (4) courage in battle, and (5) the judgment to determine when killing is or is not necessary. In forming the objectives of the hwarang, Wongwang blended Buddhist philosophy, Confucian thought, and ideas native to the region.

During the unified Silla period, literature, art, and science progressed rapidly, and virtually all of Silla society—from the royal house to the village dwellers—practiced Buddhism. Monks traveled from Korea to China and even India to study the teachings of Buddha. Various sects developed, such as Pure Land Buddhism, which was popular among the masses because it did not require that worshipers know how to read or fully comprehend the complex sutras. Some time before 751, the Silla people began using woodblock printing to reproduce sutras and Confucian writings. A surviving copy of a famous Buddhist sutra from Silla, the Dharani sutra (circa 704–51), stands as the oldest example of this style of printing.

Silla architecture also reached its peak during the reign of King Pophung. Situated among the hills near Mount Tohamsan, the Buddhist temple of Pulguksa remains one of Korea's most important national treasures. Although all of the wooden structures of the temple were destroyed during a Japanese attack in 1593, the temple grounds, which include a number of magnificent pagodas (towers built as shrines), stone bridges, and lily ponds, attest to the superior craftsmanship of Silla architects and stonemasons. The Chomsongdae Observatory, built in Kumsong (now Kyongju, South Korea) in 647, stands more than 29 feet (9 meters) high and is probably the oldest astronomical observatory still in existence in East Asia. It was a major contribution to the development of the sciences of meteorology and astronomy.

Silla society revolved around an aristocratic class structure called the "bone rank" system (*Kolpum* in Korean). A person's bone rank, or hereditary bloodline, determined what special privileges he or she would or would not receive. By the latter half of the 8th century, the aristocracy with high-ranking status began to resist the authoritarian power of the throne. Eventually the king was murdered, and the rulers during the "later period" (*hadae*) of unified Silla descended from King Wonsong, no longer from King Muyol.

By the end of the 9th century, the central government no longer had control over the activities of the "castle lords" who ruled the countryside by building fortifications around the settlements of the local population. As the castle lords became more corrupt, the central government found it increasingly difficult to collect taxes from the peasants. Around the year 889, peasant revolts began to erupt with great frequency, leading to the formation of bands of rebel armies such as the Red Trousered Banditti and "grass brigands." These revolts signaled the beginning of the end of Silla rule.

In 918, General Wang Kon made himself king of the northern region that had once been Koguryo and renamed it Koryo. He called this new era *Chonsu*, which means "Heaven's Mandate." Meanwhile, Kyonhwon, the leader of Later Paekche region, invaded Silla's capital and killed King Kyongae. Wang Kon then led forces into Silla and overtook Kyonhwon's army. He united the peninsula under Koryo rule, and by 936, the Koryo dynasty had fully emerged.

The Koryo Dynasty

The dynasty created by Wang Kon lasted until the end of the 14th century. During this period in Korean history, local landowners and the merchant class gained power, and Pyongyang became an important military center as the new regime prepared to defend itself against invasion from the tribes in the north. The peninsula was divided into provinces, but the central government still appointed the governors of these regions. In 958, King Wang Kon established a civil service examination system to recruit officials on the basis of their education. This system was developed to strengthen royal authority over the military. Chinese and Japanese pirates continued to cause disturbances on the south and east coasts, but it was the Khitan people in power in Manchuria who threatened the stability of Koryo most profoundly.

After conquering Paekche in 926, the Khitan became known as the Liao. From 1010 to 1020, the Liao tribe waged war with Koryo, burning the capital city of Kaegyong (now Kaesong). But Koryo freed itself from Liao forces and enjoyed almost a whole century of peace and prosperity. A new aristocratic class evolved called the *yangban*, which is the term that Koreans continue to use to describe the upper class. This new class consisted of members of families who were directly involved in the creation of the Koryo state. They received many privileges, including landholdings and tax exemptions.

International trade also flourished during the Koryo dynasty. Koryo traded with several nearby states, including China under the Sung rulers, Liao, Japan, the Jurchen tribes in eastern Manchuria, and even the Arabs, who traded perfumes, dyes, and drugs for Korean silk, gold, and ceramics.

A celadon jar with an incised design of a flower shows the highly developed state of pottery during the 12th century (Koryo dynasty). Even at this early date, Korean celadon ware had an international reputation for its great beauty and technique.

The 12th century ushered in a new phase of internal struggles and revolts. Local rebellions against the central government led to its complete overthrow, called a *coup d'état*, in 1170. The military then ruled the country for more than 60 years.

In 1231, an aggressive faction of Mongols from the Manchurian plains and central Asia invaded Koryo. Koryo forces resisted the Mongol advances, but they were no match for the mounted troops from the north, and in 1232 the Koryo court and officials ran away to the island of Kangwhado. Successive Koryo kings were forced to marry Mongol princesses, and the Mongol influence affected all aspects of Koryo life. Under Kublai Khan, the Mongol emperor of China, the Mongols enlisted thousands of Korean men and ships to invade Japan, first in 1274 and then again in 1281. But in the summer of 1281 a tropical typhoon, which the Japanese called the *kamikaze*, or "divine wind," destroyed Kublai Khan's fleet and killed more than half of his troops. (To the Japanese, the typhoon had been a message from the gods, telling them that Japan would not fall into the enemy's hands.)

Koryo adopted much of the advanced technology and culture of China's Sung and Yüan dynasties. Following the Sung dynasty's lead, Koryo made advances in printing and publishing,

These woodblocks—more than 80,000 in all—were used to print the Tripitaka Koreana, a Buddhist sutra, after the Koryo court was forced to flee to the island of Kangwhado by the Mongols in 1238. One of the most significant inventions in printing of the Koryo period was the movable cast metal type in 1234.

initially using woodblock printing to publish books for its growing libraries. Records show that as early as 1234, movable cast metal type was used in Koryo, making Korea the first country in the world to use this method of printing. Although the German artisan Johannes Gutenberg is credited in the West as the first to print from movable type (1450), Koryo's printing technique preceded Gutenberg by more than 200 years.

The twin tombs of King Kongmin, the 31st king of Koryo, and his wife are located in Kaesong. Built between 1365 and 1372, the terraces of the tomb complex include granite statues of civil officials, military officers, sheep, and tigers.

Medical knowledge also advanced during the 13th century. The Sung dynasty influenced Korea in this area, but Koryo medicine also developed from local Korean folk remedies. Many books on medical science were published during this time, including *Emergency Remedies of Folk Medicine* and *Folk Remedies of Samhwaja*.

The manufacture of gunpowder was another industry that came to Koryo by way of the Yüan of China. China had kept its method of production a secret since the time of the Sung dynasty. Choe Mu-son, a minor Koryo government official, discovered this closely guarded secret around 1377 and convinced the Koryo court to create a Superintendency for Gunpowder Weapons in order to make cannons and other gun weaponry. This development greatly strengthened Korea's military might.

During the Later Koryo period (the 14th century), Koreans followed the Yüan example and began cultivating cotton. Until this time, Koreans had used hemp mainly to make their clothes; only the aristocracy used ramie and silk. The use of cotton became widespread during the Yi dynasty of the Choson kingdom (1392–1910).

By the early 14th century, the Mongol empire had begun to crumble. The Chinese Ming dynasty managed to push the Mongols back to the far north, and Korea regained its independence. In 1359 and again in 1361, Chinese rebel armies called Red Banner bandits invaded Koryo and burned and sacked Kaegyong. General Yi Song-gye, one of Koryo's powerful military commanders, took orders to attack Ming forces in the Liaodong region of Manchuria. But instead, he revolted at the Yalu River and turned his army against his own capital, which was then Kaegyong. He seized the city and took the throne in 1392, thus creating what turned out to be Korea's longest reigning dynasty—the Yi dynasty. General Yi called himself King Taejo, renamed the state Choson after the first Korean kingdom 15 centuries earlier, and made Hanyang (present-day Seoul) the capital of his realm.

The Yi Dynasty

The dynasty founded by General Yi Song-gye lasted until the beginning of the 20th century, making it one of the most enduring regimes ever in existence. Immense intellectual and cultural developments characterized the period. The Buddhist state, with its military leaders holding the primary power, yielded to the thinking of the new Choson kingdom, a kingdom ruled by civilians who devotedly followed Confucian principles. King Taejo and his followers put in force extensive land reforms, such as guaranteeing land tenure to the peasants so that land could not be confiscated from them. King Taejo also developed a close relationship with China's new Ming dynasty (1368–1662), adopting a policy known as *sadae chuui*, or "bending before the great." The Yi government, for example, sent three emissaries to China each year: The first was sent to wish the Ming rulers well on New Year's Day, the second went to honor the emperor's birthday, and the third was dispatched to wish the imperial crown prince well on his birthday.

The yangban class—composed of privileged scholars and office-holding aristocrats—ruled the government, economy, and culture of Yi society. King Taejong, Taejo's fifth son, reigned in the early years of the 15th century. He made sweeping changes, such as banning private armies, centralizing the government, and forbidding Buddhist worship—he closed all but 242 Buddhist temples. Some Yi kings were Buddhists—including the fourth ruler, King Sejong (1418–50), who initiated many advances in art, science, and technology—but Buddhism no longer had any real influence on the structure of society. In spite of this, no single organized religion replaced it. Although people still believed in shamanism, fortune-telling, and superstitions, Korea essentially became a secular, not a religious, society.

In the early 15th century, King Sejong, called Sejong the Great, appointed young scholars to the Hall of Worthies to do research to advance technology. They produced a variety of important inventions, the most essential of which was the *hunmin chongum*, the Korean alphabet now known as *hangul*, "the great writing." Completed in 1446 and containing 28 letters (11 vowels and 17 consonants), hangul was devised so that all of King Sejong's people could learn to read and write. Prior to this time, Chinese characters had been used for writing by the Korean aristocracy—the only people with the time or education to memorize the tens of thousands of characters. (Today hangul contains 21 vowels and 19 consonants.) The Hall of Worthies also invented a gauge for measuring rainfall, which enabled Korea to develop a tax system based on the different amounts of precipitation around the country.

Korea experienced a political decline at the end of the 15th century. Members of the yangban quarreled over minor points of Confucian etiquette and ritual, and corruption ran rampant in the civil service. Royal relatives increased their landholdings, and because many of them were exempt from taxes, the amount of collected state revenues decreased. The state then overtaxed the farmers. The factional conflict within the yangban class continued for most of the 16th century. During this time, radical Confucian scholars called *Sarim-pa* attempted to restructure Korea into their image of a perfect Confucian society. They developed a social contract for the villages called the *hyangyak*, which encouraged villages to use the detailed codes to regulate village and family behavior. These codes emphasized morality, supervision of misconduct, etiquette, and willingness to aid others during hard times. The Sarim-pa generally monitored the villages' use of the hyangyak, giving them more power over rituals than that held by the local officials who had been appointed by the central government.

In 1592, Toyotomi Hideyoshi, the military governor of Japan (known as a *shogun*), invaded Korea in order to attain a pas-

A Japanese print depicts Japan's invasion of Korea in 1592. Toyotomi Hideyoshi, the Japanese shogun, captured Seoul in retaliation for Korea's refusal to help him attack China. With the assistance of Chinese troops, Korea forced the Japanese to evacuate the capital and flee southward.

sageway to launch an attack on the Ming empire of China. The Japanese armies reached Seoul in no time and proceeded to trample the entire countryside. Local populations blamed the government for not protecting them. Korean Admiral Yi Sun-sin did, however, seize control of the seas using his notorious "turtle ships" (*kobukson*), which had protective iron spikes and coverings for repelling enemy arrows and shells. With the help of guerrilla forces who made surprise attacks on the Japanese and a Ming relief army of 50,000 troops, Korea eventually forced the Japanese southward.

Japan attacked again in 1597, but Korea was prepared this time. By 1598, Hideyoshi had died, and the Japanese withdrew from the peninsula that same year. But the war with Japan left Korea in tatters; the land had been devastated, and government records and countless works of art had been destroyed.

During the 17th century, Korea found itself drawn into a bloody war between the Ming and the Manchu while struggling to contain factional fighting within its own borders. Meanwhile, Western influences began to make their way from other East Asian countries. Christianity, for instance, reached Korea by way of China. One of the first recorded direct contacts Korea had with the Western world occurred in 1653, when 36 survivors of a shipwreck off Cheju Island were brought to Seoul. Eight of the Dutch sailors escaped 13 years later, and one of them, Hendrick Hamel, left behind an account of his experiences in Korea. Hamel's story was the first book about Korea published in the West.

By 1785, the Korean government had taken extreme measures to expel Roman Catholic missionaries, who were seen as a threat to Confucian teachings. The government banned all forms of Western learning. This closed-door policy lasted until the 1880s. During the early 19th century, European ships touched Korean shores, but Korea refused to trade with those aboard.

Western ideas, however, did find their way into Korea, mainly through works written by European Jesuit missionaries living in China under the Ming. These ideas, coupled with frustration over the social and economic depression of the 17th and 18th centuries, spawned a new intellectual movement called *Sirhak*, which means "School of Practical Learning." First developed by the Confucian scholar Yi Su-gwang (1563–1628), Sirhak supported the idea of using knowledge for practical purposes. Advocated by discontented scholars, ex-officials, and so-called commoners, it directly opposed the dominant thought of neo-Confucianism, which stressed abstract, classical Confucian teachings. Sirhak scholars placed a strong emphasis on the study of Korean history. In an effort to achieve a better understanding of their own land, they wrote numerous texts and encyclopedias, including *Classified Dictionary of the Grassy Peak* (1614), which described the countries of

A painting (on silk) illustrates the defense of Tongnae Fortress during the reign of King Yongjo. King Yongjo, who ruled from 1724 to 1776, tried to end fighting among scholars, officials, soldiers, and peasants by seeking their advice, by revising taxes, and by publishing books in Korean to educate the people.

Europe and Southeast Asia and explained the nature of Catholicism for the first time. During the reigns of Yongjo (1725–75) and Chongjo (1776–1800), the scholars of Sirhak reached their height of popularity when both kings supported the preparation of works on government administration and law.

During the 19th century, Western countries continued efforts to establish contact with Korea. Britain, France, the United States, Russia, and others came to Korean shores primarily for trading purposes. In 1832, an English merchant ship landed off the coast of Chungchong province, and in 1846, three French warships landed there and left a note to be given to the Korean court. In 1854, two armed Russian ships sailed along the Hamgyong coast and murdered a few Koreans along the way. And in 1866, the

American trading ship *General Sherman*, hoping to open Korean ports to trade, sailed up the Taedong River to Pyongyang. There they were welcomed by an enraged mob of Koreans who, in retaliation for the crew's recklessness, set fire to the ship, killing all aboard.

Part of Korea's strongly negative reaction to outsiders stemmed from its awareness of China's troubles with Western nations, particularly the devastation endured by the Chinese during the First Opium War of 1839–42. Throughout the late 18th and early 19th centuries, British traders illegally smuggled opium from India into China. When the Chinese government attempted to ban this activity, Britain retaliated by sinking 29 Chinese junks (flat-bottomed boats). The Chinese army was no match for the British navy, and Britain easily won the war and successfully opened China's doors to more extensive trading.

Korea also greatly feared the spread of Catholicism. When it reached the peasant populations, the court responded with the Catholic Persecution of 1801, and Korean Catholics were either banned from the country or executed for promoting worship that went against native rites and beliefs. These persecuted people were labeled heretics.

The last powerful leader of traditional Korea, Taewon-gun, better known as Prince Regent Yi Ha-ung (1820–98), was a staunch isolationist. His control over the country lasted until 1873, when Confucian officials drove him out of power. China and Japan had already undergone widespread reform as a result of Western influences. In 1854, U.S. commodore Matthew C. Perry traveled to Japan, and his visit launched Japan on the road to modernization. With the removal of Taewon-gun, the antiforeigner tide began to change in Korea. Japan was able to force a Western-style treaty—the Treaty of Kanghwa—on the Korean government, by which it opened up three Korean ports for trade with Japan. Other treaties followed, including one with the United States in 1882, one with

Officials from Korea and Great Britain sign a trade agreement in 1883. Korea's treaties with the West and Japan during the late 19th century not only put Korea on the road to economic and social modernization but also opened the door to aggressive political activities by outsiders.

Britain and one with the German Empire in 1883, and one with Italy, Russia, and others soon after that.

Meanwhile, Japanese attempts to modernize Korea placed Japan in direct conflict with China, which had for centuries played a substantial role in Korea's development. By the end of the 1880s, China, Japan, and Russia had more interest in Korea than any of the Western countries had. Progressive Koreans looked to Japan as a model of how Korea itself could become modernized. The Korean court, however, was extremely conservative. In 1884, the progressives led a revolt against the court. Responding to the Korean court's desperate cry for help, the Chinese government sent troops to the peninsula and successfully forced the Japanese out of Seoul. Under the Tientsin Agreement of 1885, which was negotiated after this dispute, China and Japan both agreed to withdraw their troops from Korea. The agreement lasted nine years.

During this time, a religious movement known as *Tonghak*, or "Eastern Learning," gained prominence. It incorporated important elements of traditional Korean religion and called for an end to corruption in the government and to the exploitation of the farmer.

In 1894 and again in 1895, a series of violent peasant revolts led by leaders of the Tonghak sect erupted. The Korean court called on China to help suppress the rebellion. Japan took advantage of this chaotic time by returning to the peninsula with troops and declaring war on China. Known as the First Sino-Japanese War ("Sino" means Chinese), it lasted less than a year. Japan easily defeated the Chinese troops, and under the Treaty of Shimonoseki signed on April 17, 1895, China gave Korea full independence. Japan ignored China's agreement with Korea and forced strict reform measures on the Korean government, including the abolition of class distinctions, the end of the civil service examination system, and the creation of a new tax system. Later that year, the Japanese minister to Korea successfully plotted the murder of King Kojong's wife, Queen Min. Kojong turned to Russia for financial support and protection.

In 1894, Japanese soldiers cart off loot taken from a Chinese city during the First Sino-Japanese War. Although China had given Korea its independence in 1895, Japan refused to honor the agreement after defeating China in 1895 and forced strict reform measures on the Korean government.

Russia's involvement in Korea turned into 10 years of frustrating struggle with Japan to gain ultimate control of the peninsula. The Russian and Japanese conflict ended in war, and Korea, which seemed like a pawn in a chess game because it was moved about at the will of the foreign powers, suffered the consequences. The beginning of the 20th century also signaled the end of the once dynamic and powerful 500-year rule of the Yi dynasty.

Japanese soldiers operate one of the giant guns used to destroy Port Arthur and the Russian ships docked there on February 8, 1904. Russia suffered a humiliating defeat by Japan in the Russo-Japanese War, a defeat that may have triggered the Russian Revolution of 1905.

4

The Japanese Occupation and the 38th Parallel

Through the Treaty of Shimonoseki of 1895, Japan had secured rights to the Liaodong Peninsula, along with Formosa (now called Taiwan) and the Pescadores Islands, from China. But shortly after the treaty was signed, Russia, which had strong interests in expanding its Trans-Siberian Railroad through Manchuria, China, and Korea, bullied Japan into returning the Liaotung Peninsula to China. Then, in 1898, in the Third Russo-Japanese Treaty, Russia bargained its way into a 25-year lease of the peninsula—most specifically, the lease of Port Arthur as a naval base. Japan and Russia eyed one another suspiciously for the next six years as each country plotted to gain control over Manchuria and Korea; neither was willing to give up ground in its struggle to control the region.

Finally, on February 8, 1904, Japanese forces attacked an unsuspecting Russian fleet anchored in the harbor of Port Arthur. Japan easily defeated the Russian navy and captured the port. Although Korea had declared itself neutral in the Russo-Japanese War, it was forced to become involved. On February 23, Japan sent

*On September 5, 1905,
U.S. president Theodore
Roosevelt (center), who
mediated the peace con-
ference after the Russo-
Japanese War, poses with
the Russian repre-
sentatives (left) and the
Japanese representatives
(right) at the peace treaty's
signing in Portsmouth,
New Hampshire. Russia
acknowledged Japanese in-
terests in Korea and Japan,
but soon after the war
Japan maneuvered itself to
take full control of the
peninsula.*

troops into Seoul and coerced the Korean government into signing the Korea-Japan Protocol so that Japan could carry out its
plans for war. Then, in September, Japan declared military control
over the entire country.

All year long Russia suffered defeat after defeat in the war with
Japan, and after a disastrous battle in the Tsushima Strait at the
close of May 1905, the end of the war drew near. In August, U.S.
president Theodore Roosevelt arranged a peace conference in
Portsmouth, New Hampshire, and by September, the Treaty of
Portsmouth was signed by both countries. Russia acknowledged
Japanese political, military, and economic interests in Korea and
turned over to Japan the Liaodong Peninsula, the southern part of
the East China railroad (which ran through Manchuria), and half
of the island of Sakhalin. Both countries also agreed to return

Manchuria to China. The United States and Britain also acquiesced to Japan's interests in Korea.

At the end of the Russo-Japanese War, Korea became Japan's protectorate, a relationship in which protection and control are assumed by a superior power over a dependent country. This development signaled the beginning of the Japanese occupation of Korea. When Korean officials refused to sign the treaty Japan had drawn up for them in November, Japanese troops surrounded the palace in Seoul and forced the Korean emperor and his cabinet to sign. Koreans refer to this document simply as the Treaty of 1905. It gave Japan full authority over all aspects of Korea's foreign relations; it prevented the Korean government from signing any treaties with other governments; and it designated the appointment of a Japanese resident-general to hold the position directly under the Korean emperor, to control Korea's foreign relations, and to carry out colonial rule.

The Treaty of 1905 outraged the Korean people. Although Japan censored the news media, the Korean press managed to rally public support against the treaty. Protests were staged everywhere. The military aide-de-camp to the king, Min Yong-hwan, wrote an impassioned letter to the nation and then committed suicide. One by one, other officials followed Min's lead. Guerrilla forces, known as "righteous armies," gathered together to resist Japanese rule. But none of these protests changed Japanese policy. King Kojong still would not accept the treaty. He tried to send Korean officials to the Second Hague Peace Conference in June 1907 to protest the injustice being done to the Korean people. Ironically, the president of the conference ruled that Korea was not entitled to participate because as a protectorate of Japan it had lost authority over its foreign relations.

Although the Korean mission to The Hague failed, the incident received worldwide attention, and Japan reacted to these events by placing a firmer grip on Korea. One of its retaliatory acts was to force Kojong to step down from the throne. Japanese officials agreed to allow Kojong's son, Sunjong, to rule as prince regent, but when Kojong consented to this plan, he did not realize that he would actually be relinquishing the Korean throne itself. Sunjong became the last emperor of the Yi dynasty in July 1907.

The Japanese continued to implement stronger regulations in Korea. They took complete charge of the government by placing a Japanese vice-minister in each department. They dismantled the Korean army and police and took over the judicial system and prisons. Even the Korean currency came under Japan's control. Korea became a mere puppet nation with none of its authority left.

Korea as a Japanese Colony

In May 1910, Japan made General Terauchi Masatake the new resident-general and gave him orders to annex Korea officially to Japan. On August 29, Japan forced Sunjong to issue a statement that he was giving up the throne and the country. On that day, against the will of the entire population, Korea became a Japanese colony. The signed statement declared that the purpose of Japanese annexation of Korea was to encourage the common goodwill between the two nations and to ensure peace in Asia.

During its 35 years as a Japanese colony, Korea experienced major economic and social developments, such as soil improvement, updated methods of farming, and industrialization in the north. Japan modernized the country along Western lines, but only Japan reaped the resulting economic benefits. Japan used the Korean economy to provide raw materials for the growing Japanese industry and to supply rice for Japanese workers. Between 1912 and 1931, the amount of rice exported to Japan increased more than 500 percent. Korean workers had to eat barley and imported millet so that there would be enough rice to export. During the occupation, northern Korea became highly industrial-

Top: *An old street in Seoul shows the open sewage system that was being used in Korea during the first decade of the 20th century.* Bottom: *During its 35 years of Korean occupation, Japan helped modernize city streets, such as the one pictured here.*

Prince Yi of Korea, the former emperor, was forced to relinquish his authority under the Japanese governor-general who ruled Korea. Prince Yi died in 1926 and was buried in Seoul.

ized, whereas the southern half remained largely agricultural. Japan relied heavily on Korea's natural resources, especially the rich source of minerals found in the northern mountain ranges. Korea was forced to supply Japan with everything from soybeans, cotton, fruits, and raw silk to coal, iron ore, magnesite, graphite, mica, cobalt, and boron. Japan owned all of the banks, all of the large industry—including steel production, utilities, shipbuilding, and mining—and most of the farmland in Korea.

(continued on page 73)

SCENES OF
NORTH KOREA

Overleaf: *Workers assemble pots in a factory in Pyongyang. Many of the factories involved with light industry, such as textiles, foodstuffs, and domestic appliances, use locally available raw materials.*

Left: *The Pyongyang Shoemaking Factory is a modern, centrally run manufacturing plant. The factory produces a variety of shoes made of materials such as leather, artificial leather, canvas, and vinyl.*

Workers gather printed fabrics in the Pyongyang Textile Combine Factory. The North Korean textile industry produces chemical fabrics—vinalon, staple fiber, orlon, and movilon—and natural fibers such as cotton, silk, and wool.

Kayaking teams train for a regatta on the Taedong River in Pyongyang.

Runners compete for the Mangyongdae Prize, an international marathon held annually in Pyongyang.

A panoramic view of Pyongyang shows the fish-shaped Light Sports Gymnasium (center), the Kim Il Sung Stadium (left foregound), and a tourist hotel (right foreground).

People read and work on their research at the Grand People's Study House in Pyongyang. The building has a total floor space of 1,076,390 square feet (100,000 square meters) and has the potential of storing 30 million books.

Children play in the Mangyongdae wading pool.

Deep-sea fishing is a vital industry along the east coast of North Korea. The major fishing ports are Wonsan and Sinpo.

(continued from page 64)

Japan ruled the country through a governor-general, who replaced the earlier resident-general. The Japanese emperor appointed the governor-general, who in turn appointed all government officials. Virtually all positions of authority were held by the Japanese, whereas the Koreans were given clerical and other minor posts. A ruling class of Japanese immigrants who held the high-ranking posts grew to astronomical proportions, reaching well over 700,000 by 1940. Japan intended to assimilate Koreans into its dominion, forcing Japanese culture and way of life on the Korean people. The Japanese government even demanded that Koreans take on Japanese names and speak only Japanese. The Japanese employed police and their own army to enforce the oppressive rules.

Until 1921, Koreans were prohibited from publishing their own newspapers or forming political or intellectual groups. But the Koreans found other ways of resisting Japanese rule. Korean nationalism was strong during the occupation, and Japanese authorities constantly fought to suppress it, usually by force. On March 1, 1919, a group of 33 prominent Koreans in Seoul issued a proclamation of independence. Roughly 500,000 Koreans—including members of religious groups—organized demonstrations in the streets, protesting against Japanese rule. The crusade, which became known as the March 1st Movement, lasted about two months. According to conservative estimates from Japanese reports, the Japanese police killed 7,509 Koreans, wounded 15,961, and imprisoned another 46,948 in the process of suppressing the movement.

The Japanese government realized, after the March 1st Movement, that it would have to change some of its policies toward Korea, or at least appear to change them. It was now apparent to the rest of the world that the Korean people had not willingly submitted to the Japanese occupation. Consequently, Japan appointed a new governor-general, Admiral Saito Makoto, who promised to issue various reforms. These reforms included expansion of the educational system for Koreans to make it equal to that available to the Japanese, freedom of speech, nondiscrimination in the appointment of officials, demilitarization of the police (in other words, the Japanese military would no longer control the police), and greater freedom of the press, which would allow the publication of Korean-owned newspapers in the hangul alphabet. Most of these promises, however, never materialized. The police force actually expanded; the promise of educational opportunities never became a reality; discrimination against Koreans persisted in the appointing of officials; and although Korean newspapers in hangul did appear, the Japanese strictly censored them.

Meanwhile, Koreans living outside of the peninsula joined together to push for Korean independence. Koreans in Siberia, Manchuria, China, and the United States formed a provisional Korean government in Shanghai in April 1919. Unlike the traditional system of government, known as a monarchy, that had served Korea for centuries, this new provisional government was to be a republic. It would allow all citizens to vote for officials to run the government. Syngman Rhee, who eventually became the first president of South Korea, was among the Koreans who set up this government. Although the organization did not change Japanese rule, it kept alive the hope for independence, as did the spirit of the protesters within the country.

In China and Manchuria, Korean nationalists also resisted Japanese rule, often by using guerrilla tactics. Some of the more successful organizations of this type included Kim Won-bong's *Uiyoltan* (Righteous Brotherhood) and Kim Ku's *Aeguktan* (Patriot Corps). Groups such as these carried out numerous bombings and attacks throughout the 1920s and 1930s, including the attempted assassination of the Japanese emperor in 1932 by Yi Pong-chang of the Aeguktan.

The USS Shaw *is ablaze after the Japanese bombed Pearl Harbor, Hawaii, on December 7, 1941. The surprise attack plunged the United States into World War II. The Korean provisional government based in Shanghai fought alongside the Allies during the war.*

During this period, another Korean living outside of the peninsula was making a name for himself as a rebel. Kim Song-ju was born in 1912 near Pyongyang and spent most of his childhood in Manchuria. In 1930 he took the pseudonym Kim Il Sung, and he purportedly organized the first anti-Japanese guerrilla unit in Antu, Manchuria, on April 25, 1932. North Koreans still celebrate this day as the founding date of the Korean People's Army. Kim's revolutionary activites eventually led him back to Korea, where he became North Korea's first president.

By the time Japan attacked Pearl Harbor, Hawaii, on December 7, 1941, bringing the United States into World War II, the Korean provisional government finally had its chance to make a stand against Japan. On December 8, the Korean provisional government declared war on Japan and formed the Restoration Army, which fought alongside the Allies in the Pacific theater of World War II.

The 38th Parallel

The conclusion of World War II brought an end to the Japanese occupation of Korea, but it also divided the peninsula into two separate countries. At the Cairo Conference held in December 1943, British prime minister Winston Churchill, U.S. president Franklin D. Roosevelt, and Chinese premier Chiang Kai-shek proclaimed that Korea would become free and independent "in due course." As World War II drew to a close, the United States and the Soviet Union agreed at the Yalta Conference in February 1945 that Japanese forces would surrender the portion of Korea north of the 38th Parallel to the Soviet Union and the part south of that line to the United States.

When Japan surrendered on August 15, 1945, Koreans took to the streets in celebration of the end of 36 years under oppressive rule, firmly believing they would gain immediate independence. But following the agreement made at the Yalta Conference, the Soviet Union arrived in northern Korea and occupied Pyongyang, Hamhung, and other major northern cities. By September 8, U.S. forces arrived in Inchon to station troops in southern Korea. This division, which was supposed to have been a temporary measure, remains a source of turbulence and tragedy for the Korean people today.

All efforts to establish a unified Korea failed in the intervening months. Moreover, a number of postwar international decisions were made without the consent of the Korean people. The Soviet

Union immediately created a provisional Communist government in northern Korea. The United States, likewise, set up a provisional republican form of government in the south.

Internal conflict grew, and on August 15, 1948, the Republic of Korea was founded south of the 38th Parallel, ostensibly to make the provisional government in Shanghai legitimate. Ten days later, the newly formed Communist party organized elections for a Supreme People's Assembly (SPA) both in the north and the south. The Democratic People's Republic of Korea (North Korea) was established on September 9, 1948, with Kim Il Sung as premier. It signed several agreements with the Soviets to provide military, economic, and technological assistance. The Soviet Union withdrew its occupation forces in December, and U.S. troops left the south in June 1949. Both North and South Korea claimed authority over the entire peninsula, and it was only a matter of time before a major collision would occur.

In February 1951, an Allied soldier looks over a Russian-made tank that collapsed a bridge near Suwon, Korea. After North Korea's surprise attack on the south, the United Nations sent troops to assist South Korea in its fight against the Communist military.

5

The Forgotten War

For most Americans today, the Korean War (1950–53) recalls memories only of the comedy series "M*A*S*H," which was originally televised on CBS from 1972 to 1983 and set during the Korean War. It has become known as the Forgotten War. But it was a major episode in 20th-century American history, postwar world history (meaning after World War II), and was perhaps *the* most tragic period in modern history for the Korean people.

No one can say with any real certainty which specific event triggered the Korean War. Both North and South Korea tempted fate by crossing the border at various points along the 38th Parallel months before North Korea's surprise attack on June 25, 1950. Internal political turmoil also plagued both sides. North Korean premier Kim Il Sung considered military force the only way to reunify the two Koreas. He hoped that by aggressively pursuing reunification, he would both resolve his differences with the Communists living south of the 38th Parallel and straighten out his ailing two-year economic plan.

In 1949, the Workers' party of North Korea and the Workers' party of South Korea (which were both Communist political parties) united to form the Korean Workers' party (KWP), and Kim Il Sung became its chairman. But it was Pak Hon-yong, the vice-premier and foreign minister of North Korea, who maintained the widest popular support among the various Communist factions in Korea, especially in the south. Both Kim and Pak sought a military solution to unite the peninsula, but for different reasons. Pak hoped to gain ultimate power in the south by initiating a North Korean attack of South Korea. Despite their differences, however, both men hoped that a forceful reunification would ease the political and economic turmoil on the peninsula.

Likewise, South Korean president Syngman Rhee made it known that he intended "to march North" in order to reunify Korea under his rule. But the North Korean military had as many as 10 infantry divisions consisting of 120,000 troops, 242 tanks, and 211 planes, whereas South Korea had only 8 army divisions with roughly 60,000 men, no tanks, and no fighter planes. President Syngman Rhee knew he could not back up his words with force; Premier Kim Il Sung, on the other hand, did not hesitate to make a move.

On June 25, 1950, troops from the Democratic People's Republic of Korea caught its southern brethren completely by surprise with an attack across the 38th Parallel. They attacked at 6:00 A.M., in the pouring rain, leaving the South Koreans in a state of confusion.

Some people believe this attack was partly the result of the confused signals American leaders were giving about South Korea's place in the U.S. defense strategy in the Pacific. In January 1950, U.S. secretary of state Dean Acheson had defined the areas that the U.S. government considered important to defend, and South Korea was not included in this zone. Thus, the North Korean government may have assumed that the United States would not act to defend South Korea from a North Korean attack. In addition, because there had been so many border conflicts initiated by both sides in the preceding year, both South Korean and American officials were slow to respond to the actual invasion. It was not until mid-morning that U.S. ambassador John Muccio finally notified Washington of the invasion.

Once U.S. president Harry S. Truman heard the news, he recommended that the United Nations (UN), an international peacekeeping organization, assist South Korea. At this point, U.S. officials did not view South Korea alone as militarily significant. They did, however, firmly believe that Soviet leader Joseph Stalin had instigated the invasion. The United States did not recognize Kim Il Sung's Communist government. Truman saw North Korea as essentially part of the Soviet Union and, therefore, controlled by Stalin. As a result, Truman and his advisers found it necessary to do everything in their power to stop Stalin's plan to use North Korea to spread communism to the free world. This extreme hostility toward Communist governments became known as the "cold war" mentality of the United States. Today most American historians think that it is unlikely that Stalin planned the invasion. They believe Kim Il Sung had very definite plans as to how to reunify Korea under a Communist government, and he saw the invasion as the first step.

By June 26, as the North Korean troops approached Seoul, Syngman Rhee and government officials escaped farther south. Meanwhile, the UN met to determine its strategy in handling the Korean crisis. On June 27, the UN—which had been created in 1945 to promote world peace—did something utterly uncharacteristic: It decided to use armed force to put an end to the conflict. Sixteen member nations of the UN—including France, Belgium, the Netherlands, Britain, Canada, Greece, Turkey, and, most significantly, the United States—supplied combat units to aid South Korea. By the end of the day on June 28, General Douglas MacArthur, who was in charge of the UN Command forces, received the report that Seoul was in enemy hands. (MacArthur was the army general whom the U.S. government had put in charge of the American occupation of Japan after World War II.) Forty-eight hours later, MacArthur received authorization to bring the troops into Korea.

President Truman, however, made the decision to commit U.S. troops without the approval of Congress (which, according to the U.S. Constitution, has the sole authority to declare war), and he refused to call the operation a war. He referred to the conflict, which would last three grueling years and leave more than 1 million soldiers and close to 1 million Korean civilians dead, as a "police action."

Over the course of the summer, North Korean forces reached the southeast corner of the peninsula before U.S. troops outnumbered them. On September 15, MacArthur launched an assault by sea, targeted to come ashore at Inchon on the west coast of South Korea, a few miles east of Seoul. American troops recaptured

Soldiers in the Chinese People's Volunteer Army prepare to defend their border with Korea in 1951. With the help of the Chinese troops, North Korea pushed UN forces south beyond Seoul.

Seoul from North Korea two weeks later. By November, South Korea's counteroffensive reached the Yalu River along the northern border between North Korea and Manchuria. But 300,000 Chinese forces and 65,000 North Korean troops surprised Mac-Arthur and his army at the border. With the aid of the Chinese People's Volunteers, North Korea pushed its enemy south again, beyond the city of Seoul.

By the spring of 1951, the field of battle settled around the 38th Parallel, and it remained there until the end of the war in 1953. Although peace talks began in the summer of 1951, the war did not officially end until July 27, 1953, in the town of Panmunjom, when the military leaders of North Korea, the Chinese People's Volunteers, and the UN Command signed an armistice. The document was created to serve as a truce until there was agreement on a permanent resolution.

The armistice designated a cease-fire line along the 38th Parallel and established the surrounding 2.5-mile-wide (4-kilometer-wide) DMZ, which remains the boundary between the two

In North Korea, the Chinese People's Volunteers stop the U.S. Marines on an icy trail in subzero temperatures during the Korean War. The war ended in Panmunjom with the signing of an armistice on July 27, 1953.

Koreas. An international conference met in Geneva in April 1954 to resolve the issue of reunification, but after seven weeks the meeting ended with the fate of the Korean people still undetermined.

The war left the peninsula a wasteland. An estimated 4 million soldiers were killed or wounded, and approximately 1 million civilians died. More than one-third of South Korea's housing was destroyed, along with a substantial number of the country's

In 1954, Korean refugees begin rebuilding their homes in an area north of the 38th Parallel. The war left the peninsula a virtual wasteland, and families had to go to work immediately to construct homes and plant crops to resettle the country.

public buildings, roads, bridges, and ports. North Korea suffered continuous aerial bombings that caused the torturous death of thousands of civilians, demolished industry, agriculture, railroads, and left only the chimneys of buildings standing.

Both Koreas moved swiftly to rebuild after the war. North Korea, under Premier Kim Il Sung, restored the production of goods to prewar levels within three years. During the 1960s, the country greatly expanded production in the iron, steel, shipbuilding, and mining industries. But it has suffered economic hardships since the mid-1970s, including food shortages and default on trade-related loans.

The Great Leader, the late Kim Il Sung (wearing hat), and his son Kim Jong Il (far left) inspect educational facilities at a school in Pyongyang. Under President Kim Il Sung's guidance, North Korea restored the production of goods to prewar levels within three years and made the education of its people one of its highest priorities.

As stipulated in the 1953 armistice agreement, the Military Armistice Commission continues to meet about once a month at Panmunjom to ensure that all parties involved adhere to the terms of the agreement. China withdrew its troops from North Korea in 1958, but approximately 43,000 U.S. troops remain stationed in South Korea. U.S. president Jimmy Carter proposed a "phased withdrawal" of the U.S. forces on the peninsula in February 1977 but reversed the decision in 1979 when he heard reports that North Korea maintained a larger military force than previously estimated.

No longer a war-torn, poverty-stricken country, defenseless against its northern neighbor, South Korea has become one of the world's leading trading nations. It competes successfully in automobile, computer, and construction markets and has opened the doors to trade with China, a long-time ally of North Korea. Many believe that this shift in the balance of power on the peninsula has made U.S. military support in South Korea unnecessary.

Since the Korean War ended in 1953, both Koreas have expressed a desire to reunify the peninsula, but until 1971 no direct communication occurred between the two governments. In August 1971, the two countries agreed to have their respective Red Cross units set up a proposal for reuniting the thousands of family members separated since the war. Although talks were held, no progress was made for 14 years.

In September 1985, the two Red Cross organizations arranged for a series of brief reunions in Seoul and Pyongyang for 100 members of divided families. Since then, officials from both countries have continued to discuss a variety of concerns, including the plight of the separated families, economic and trade issues, and nuclear power.

In December 1991, North and South Korea signed a pact of nonaggression and an agreement barring either country from developing, testing, or storing nuclear weapons. But the years following this hopeful declaration were tense. International inspectors were occasionally denied entrance to North Korean sites suspected of manufacturing arms, and the North Korean government withdrew from the Nuclear Non-Proliferation Treaty, protesting the United States' continued military support of the south. When Kim Il Sung died in 1994, to be succeeded by his son, foreign observers began to find the North Korean government's behavior increasingly unpredictable. Even so, talks managed to coax North Korea into freezing its own nuclear program in exchange for a nuclear power reactor from South Korea that would be used for peaceful energy purposes.

By the late 1990s, an overriding consideration was the problem of feeding the North Korean people. Record floods had turned the repeated food shortages into widespread famine. A defecting senior member of North Korea's government, Hwang Jang Yop, claimed that the north was desperate enough for food and resources that nothing, not even a new war, was out of the realm of possibility.

Members of the Supreme People's Assembly meet in Pyongyang.

6

Government

North Korea has a strongly centralized government in which the Communist Korean Workers' party (KWP) has complete power. Kim Il Sung led the North Korean Communist party in all its various forms from 1945 until his death in 1994 and held the highest-ranking position in the government. His son, Kim Jong Il, succeeded his father in power but did not formally assume office as president of the country or secretary-general of the party.

In 1947, the country's first Supreme People's Assembly (SPA) drafted a constitution, which went into effect in 1948. This document established a cabinet, headed by a premier, that would have executive power over the state. The elected SPA supposedly had control over this cabinet, but in reality, the cabinet acted on decisions made by the KWP central committee.

In December 1972, the Fifth Supreme People's Assembly approved a new constitution (amended somewhat in 1992) to give the highest-ranking member of the government more power and a larger group of advisers. This constitution instituted the selection of a president by the SPA as well as a high-level government agency called the Central People's Committee (CPC). The president of the republic, elected to four-year terms, chooses who will serve on the CPC, which includes the president, vice-presidents, and about 15 other members. The SPA, which consists of 687 elected officials, remains the highest-ranking organization in the government, but it holds this status in name only. In practice, the president and the CPC (unofficially headed by Kim Jong Il) actually control the government.

The constitution requires that the SPA be elected every 4 years by means of a general election in which all citizens who are at least 17 years of age can vote. In actuality, elections have been held irregularly, and the nominees run unopposed. According to the constitution, the CPC, under the direction of the president, makes the high-level policy decisions and oversees a cabinet called the State Administration Council. This cabinet controls the administrative and executive functions of the government, while the SPA oversees the legislative functions.

North Korea has only one political party, the Korean Workers' party. It functions as the core part of a larger group known as the Democratic Front for the Reunification of the Fatherland, which was established in 1946.

The SPA has a standing committee that appoints judges to the state's highest courts for four-year terms. The judicial system consists of the Central Court (the highest court in the country), the Court of the Province, and the People's Court. The Central Court protects state property and constitutional rights, supervises the observation of all state laws, and makes official judgments.

North Korea is divided into 13 administrative units, including 4 cities—the nation's capital Pyongyang (population 2.6 million), Chongjin (population 760,000), Hamhung (population 790,000), and Kaesong (population 350,000)—and 9 provinces. Each province has a capital city: Nampo in South Pyongan, Sinuiju in North Pyongan, Kanggye in Chagang, Haeju in South Hwanghae, Sariwon in North Hwanghae, Wonsan in Kangwon, Hamhung in

South Hamgyong, Chongjin in North Hamgyong, and Hyesan in Ryanggang. The provinces are subdivided into 152 counties. A total of 26,539 deputies serve on people's assemblies at the city/province, county, and commune levels.

Cities

Unlike many of the crowded, polluted major cities in East Asia, Pyongyang is a beautiful, clean, well-planned capital. Museums, skyscrapers, and monuments to Kim Il Sung make up the Pyong-yang skyline. The city also has modern factories with technologi-cally advanced equipment. Few people in Pyongyang own cars or even bicycles anymore. Instead, they rely heavily on the city's subway system.

Trolley bus service is available at the Pyongyang train station. Trains are the most impor-tant mode of transportation in North Korea.

Other important metropolitan areas in North Korea include the ports and industrial centers of Wonsan, Hungnam, Chongjin, and Najin on the east coast, Sinuiju at the mouth of the Yalu River, Kaesong just north of the DMZ, and Nampo just west of Pyongyang. Wonsan, Chongjin, and Nampo have been national models for rice cultivation and the fishing industry.

Transportation

The country has approximately 18,600 miles (30,000 kilometers) of highways, including four-lane highways running from Pyongyang to Nampo and from Pyongyang to Wonsan. North Korea also has over 3,000 miles (4,800 kilometers) of railroad track, and it still transports most freight by rail. The great majority of the trains run on electricity. The country has 49 airports and provides international service to Khabarovsk, Beijing, and Hong Kong and domestic service to Hamhung and Chongjin.

Military Force

Known collectively as the Korean People's Army (KPA), the North Korean armed forces have an estimated total of over 1.2 million troops. A huge proportion of these are stationed at the demilitarized zone. The army accounts for about 1 million of the total, the air force for 82,000, and the navy for 46,000. North Korea also has about 115,000 security and border troops, about 3 million "Red Guards" (a worker's militia), and approximately 700,000 members in a youth militia. According to recent estimates, the nation has been allotting a quarter or more of its gross domestic product to defense—an enormous percentage, especially for an economically struggling country. Military service is required and can be fulfilled by a 5-year term in the army or navy or a 3- to 4-year term in the air force. Kim Jong Il is de facto commander in chief of the armed forces, and the Ministry of Public Security, supervised by the KWP, manages the police.

Female students at Pyongyang Senior Middle School No. 1 listen to instructional tapes. Senior middle schools, where students (ages 10 to 16) receive 6 years of education, are similar to secondary schools in the United States.

Education, Communication, and Other Social Services

The North Korean government considers education one of its highest priorities. North Korea has a 99 percent literacy rate. (The United States has a somewhat lower literacy rate.) Education in state schools is free and compulsory, and it lasts for 11 years. Children enter kindergarten at age four and primary school at age six. Four years later they enter senior middle school for six years, where the curriculum is broadly based. For students who continue beyond the years of compulsory education, North Korea offers more than 200 institutions of higher learning, including four universities and an academy of sciences.

Part of each child's education involves political training on the importance of following a socialist way of life. This may include, for example, the study of Kim Il Sung's written works. Starting at the age of 14, children must also learn English as a second language. Despite the great importance the government places on education, the economic crisis in the late 1990s prevented the establishment of many more schools. Visitors from international agencies reported high rates of school absenteeism because of famine and illness.

The Propaganda and Agitation Department of the party controls all communication. The KWP censors and approves the hiring of staff for all news media. The official governmental news agency is the Korean Central News Agency. By 1996, the country had 11 newspapers, including *Rodong Sinmun* (Workers' Daily News), which is the official KWP newspaper and has a circulation of about 1 million; *Rodongja Sinmun*, the newspaper of the General Federation of Trade Unions; *Minju Choson* (Democratic Korea), the Supreme People's Assembly and Administration Council newspaper; *Joson Inmingun*, the Korean People's Army daily paper; *Saenal*, the biweekly Youth League paper; and *Korea Today*, a monthly paper published by the Foreign Languages Press Group in Chinese, English, French, Russian, and Spanish. In 1997 the Central News Agency also posted a World Wide Web site.

The Korean Central Broadcasting Committee manages all radio and television service. By the early 1990s, the country had 18 radio stations and 11 television stations. By the mid-1990s, there was a radio for approximately every 9 people and a television for about every 11.5 people. However, only about one person in every 21 had a telephone.

The state officially provides a variety of social programs, including free medical care. But this became difficult in the mid-1990s as cash grew scarce and medical supplies were overwhelmed by catastrophic floods. As of 1996, there were about 2,700 hospitals, but few new ones have been built recently. Estimates of the number of doctors range from 1 per 700 citizens to 1 per 370.

Sexual equality laws were enacted in 1946 but have taken a long time to enforce. Women have, for the most part, achieved equality in the workplace, but not in the home. Domestic life tends to be structured traditionally, with the women doing the cooking and cleaning. But women do make up 49 percent of the work force. Women receive five months paid maternity leave, and if a woman has three or more children, she receives eight hours of pay for six

The Grand People's Study House, located on Namsan Hill in the heart of Pyongyang, was opened to the public in 1982. The white granite building with a hip-saddle roof of blue tiles houses more than 600 rooms, including reading rooms, lecture and recording rooms, and a library.

hours of work per day. In the 1990s, there were more Korean women holding government positions than there were American women holding comparable positions in the United States.

The Cult of Kim and Chuche

North Korea has developed differently from other Communist countries for several reasons. First, it often isolated itself from the two Communist countries that played the largest roles in its historical development: China and the Soviet Union. In 1962, the North Korean government appeared to support China in a Sino-Soviet dispute over North Korea. (North Korea, like China, denounced the Soviet policy of peaceful coexistence with the West.) In 1963, Moscow withdrew its military and economic support of North Korea. But by the time of the Chinese Cultural Revolution (1966–76), North Korea had begun to free itself of pro-Chinese elements as well. On October 5, 1966, Kim Il Sung gave a speech at a party conference that established North Korea's political independence from all other Communist countries.

Another reason for North Korea's uniqueness is the fact that it had only one leader for almost four decades after its official birth as an independent socialist state. By the time of Kim Il Sung's death, Cuba was the only other Communist country whose original leader continued to rule.

In many ways, the North Korean people worshiped Kim Il Sung as a god. His countrypeople called him the "Great Leader" and his son, Kim Jong Il, the "Dear Leader." Children were taught from an early age to honor the Great Leader as the heroic father-figure who would protect them from outside evils. Even after his death, Kim Il Sung commands great reverence among the people. His huge memorial in Pyongyang receives thousands of mourners daily who pay their respects and lay wreaths.

Now the Dear Leader has taken command. Kim Jong Il had long been groomed to succeed his father, and when Kim Il Sung died in July 1994 Korea became the first historical instance of a Communist monarchy. (A monarchy is a government in which the leadership is inherited by members of the reigning family.) The country now also officially worships Kim Jong Il. Homes throughout the country have framed photographs of both men and copies of their written works. The people are told that Kim Jong Il was born on Mount Paekdu like a mythic god, instead of in Siberia as Western analysts contend. Criticism of Kim Jong Il, even in private, is likely to meet with swift punishment. Many observers believe, however, that Kim Jong Il lacks his father's enormous charisma and political skills.

The third reason North Korea has developed along a separate path is closely related to the first two reasons. Kim Il Sung constructed his own brand of Communist thought, called *chuche sasang*, which means self-reliance. From the start, Kim used chuche to rule the country, and it blossomed into the state political ideology when Kim declared North Korea's independence from both Soviet and Chinese political influence in the 1960s. Article 4 of the 1972 constitution called chuche the guiding force behind the government's activities. The constitutional revisions in 1992, though never publicized, reportedly say that the government may now create incentives to encourage innovation and investment, even from foreign sources, while still technically following chuche.

Chuche takes the theories of Karl Marx and of V. I. Lenin and applies them to the particular circumstances of North Korea. Karl Marx was a 19th-century German revolutionary thinker who founded the modern ideas of socialism and communism and worked to spread social reforms in England and Western Europe. V. I. Lenin was the leader of the Russian Communist revolution in 1917.

From the general concept of chuche, Kim developed the idea of *chaju*, which means political independence from other nations; *charip*, which refers to a self-sustaining economy that relies on the country's own workers and resources; and *chawi*, which is the principle of military self-defense. In practice, the North Korean government uses chuche to emphasize a system of national self-defense; therefore, it is viewed by political analysts as a form of nationalism, which advocates a concern for one's own country over consideration of international issues.

Perhaps the best way to view chuche is to see it in relation to the history of the Korean people. Chuche is an easily understood reaction to the repeated invasions and manipulations by foreign countries that the Korean people have had to bear since their ancestors first settled on the peninsula. But whether chuche as an ideology can survive the severe hardships of recent years is debatable. Hwang Jang Yop, the top government official whom Westerners often described as the "architect" of chuche, defected to the south in 1997, and he declared that chuche had failed.

Trains are produced at the Kim Jong Tae Electric Locomotive Factory in Pyongyang. The government plans the country's economic development in phases of three to seven years, and each phase includes specific goals for progress in industry.

7

The Economy and Foreign Relations

North Korea has a socialized, centralized, and planned economy. Its land and agricultural production is completely collectivized by the state, and state-owned industry produces more than 95 percent of the country's manufactured goods. The government has planned the country's economic development in phases of three to seven years. Each phase includes specific targets for growth in industry and agriculture, which economic experts predict the country will reach within the years covered by the plan. The government also exercises strict control over prices, wages, trade, budgets, and banking.

North Korea holds approximately 80 percent of all of the mineral deposits on the peninsula. It has an abundance of iron ore, copper, lead, zinc, uranium, and manganese. During the Japanese occupation, the northern half of the peninsula accounted for 65 percent of Korean heavy industry, including the development of hydroelectricity, the mining of raw materials, and the production of chemical fertilizers. The Korean War practically destroyed this

Workers harvest rice on a farm near Pyongyang. Agricultural production is completely collectivized by the government.

industrial base, but after the war, North Korea mobilized its work force and used its natural resources to achieve rapid economic development. Its major exports are semimanufactured metal products, magnesite powder, lead, zinc, and cement. Its major imports include machinery for industrial plants, petroleum, coal, and wheat. In 1995, heavy industry accounted for more than 60 percent of the country's national income. The country generates its energy mainly from coal and hydroelectric power.

In 1953, Pyongyang began its intense industrialization campaign, focusing on iron and steel, machine tools, shipbuilding, mining, electric power, chemicals, and building materials. The government declared the first three-year economic plan (1954–56) a resounding success. Heavy industry received about 80 percent of the available funds for industrial development, and the country attained major growth in metallurgy, machine tools, electric power, chemicals, and mining. Following a Soviet model of in-

A heavy-machinery factory in South Pyongyang province manufactures pumps and transformers. North Korea has a solid base in heavy industry, including electric power, metallurgy, engineering, and chemical and building materials.

dustrial development, North Korea reported an increase in the gross industrial production rate of 41.8 percent per year. During the subsequent five-year economic plan (1957–61), it reported an increase in its industrial production at a rate of 36.6 percent per year. Although party officials may have exaggerated these figures, the country did achieve an uncommonly high industrial growth rate during the eight years following the Korean War.

No clear data on economic development exist beyond this period, but estimates indicate that the growth rates decreased from the 1960s to the late 1980s. Around 1989, North Korea appears to have entered a period of *negative* growth—that is, its total output of goods and services, usually measured by the gross domestic product (GDP), has actually been shrinking. Estimates place the rate of decline between 1989 and 1995 at approximately 4 to 5 percent a year.

Another serious problem for North Korea's economy is the national debt. In the 1970s, trying to compete with South Korea, the north undertook a massive modernization program, especially in heavy industry. This program led to a national debt of $1.6 million by 1975. The country also owed its Communist creditors another $1 billion. In that decade, North Korea became the first Communist country to default on its loans from free-market countries. It renegotiated much of its international debt in 1979, but defaulted again in 1980. By 1993, suffering from the loss of favorable trade deals with Russia and China, North Korea had a $10 billion debt and had failed to meet many of its five-year plan's industrial targets. Disproportionate spending on defense continued to magnify the problems. Today, North Korea's credit rating with potential investors remains low, and the gap in economic growth between North and South Korea continues to widen.

The Korean Workers' party considers agriculture second to industry in importance. Complete collectivization occurred between 1954 and 1958. Cooperatives farm 90 percent of the cultivated land, and all of the land belongs either to the state or to the cooperatives. The principal crops include rice, corn, coarse grains, potatoes, other vegetables, and tobacco. Livestock farming has also become increasingly important, with most farms of this type owned by the state. The farms raise horses, cattle, pigs, sheep, goats, and chickens for meat, milk, eggs, and hides. Fisheries and forestry operations are also supported and run by the government.

Despite North Korea's efforts to modernize its agricultural production, and despite the fact that more than a third of the labor force is devoted to agriculture, the nation is still not self-sufficient in food. In the 1980s it traded zinc for wheat with India and imported rice and corn from Thailand. By the mid-1990s, with floods having wiped out much of the land's productivity, the shortfall was tremendous. Estimates placed the grain shortage at 3 million tons in 1995 and another 2 million tons in 1996. Half a million people had been displaced from their land. Soon the word *famine* was being used by concerned observers, and North Korea was forced to ask the world for humanitarian aid.

Foreign Relations and Trade

North Korea has no diplomatic relations with the United States, and reliable reports about events and conditions in North Korea have often been scarce. After the establishment of the socialist state, Western journalists were generally not welcome in the country. Until recently, in fact, only a tiny number of foreigners from Western countries visited North Korea. The government succeeded in maintaining the isolation that it desired.

Shoppers at a trade fair in Pyongyang look over consumer goods produced by North Koreans. Commodities are manufactured on a planned basis according to the needs of the people, and prices of the same goods are uniform no matter where the shops are located.

Since the late 1980s, the North Koreans have been somewhat more open to foreigners. A few cultural and academic exchanges have occurred. In 1991, realizing that its economic crisis demanded an opening to the world, North Korea joined the United Nations.

Trade has followed a similar pattern. Beginning immediately after the Korean War, the Soviet Union supplied North Korea with economic aid. In 1961, North Korea entered into treaties of friendship, cooperation, and mutual assistance with both the Soviet Union and China. Despite Kim Il Sung's proclamation of the country's independence, the Chinese and Soviets continued to exert a strong influence for decades, so that many Westerners thought of North Korea as essentially a client state of the Communist superpowers.

But in 1984, realizing its need to rejuvenate the economy, the North Korean government resolved to pursue economic arrangements with capitalist, as well as Communist, countries. A Joint Venture Law was passed, encouraging businesses from both socialist and capitalist countries to invest in North Korean enterprises. This law had mixed results. Though a number of joint ventures were developed with France, Germany, India, and other countries, almost all failed. Those that prospered were the deals with Japan-based Koreans (*Chochongnyon* Koreans). One of these deals led to the opening of Nakwon department stores in Pyongyang and other locations. North Korea also designated a "Free Economic Zone" in one province, promising relaxed regulations on employing non-Koreans and on the use of foreign currency.

Meanwhile, North and South Korea began to investigate the possibility of setting up economic links with one another. Limited trading between the two countries began in November 1988. A more direct trade began in 1990 after the two countries' prime ministers met for the first time ever. Further contacts have developed since then. Business projects have included tourism, highway development, rail links between north and south, and a proposed light industrial complex to be built in Nampo for the South Korean company Daewoo.

But through the late 1990s, business relations between the two Koreas remained somewhat volatile, to say the least. Questions about North Korea's nuclear power program led to a shutdown of investment for about a year. Then a framework was agreed upon in which North Korea would freeze its nuclear program in exchange for limited mineral trade with the United States and an easing of economic sanctions.

As the century wound to a close, North Korea had a long way to go before its level of international trade could catch up with that of its neighbors. Some economic experts have advised the North Korean government to expand its light industry. But as long as the economy remains in a downward spiral, the specific type of industry that North Korea pursues is not as important as a fundamental policy shift toward more external trade and openness to the outside world.

Tae kwon do, a self-defense martial art that originated in Korea more than 2,000 years ago, is a national sport of international renown. It has become very popular at world sports events, including the World Games and the Asian Games, and was showcased at Olympic ceremonies in 1988 and 1992.

8

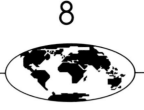

The People and Their Culture

The estimated 70 million people living on the Korean peninsula are racially and linguistically homogeneous. Approximately 24 million of those people live in North Korea. They are the ethnic descendants of a Tungusic branch of the Ural-Altaic family, and their spoken language is Korean. It is a Uralic language with similarities to Japanese, Mongolian, Hungarian, and Finnish.

Just as the history of outside aggression helped shape the chuche political and economic ideas, it also has greatly influenced Korean culture. Aspects of Chinese, Indian, Japanese, and Western cultures have filtered into Korean society throughout its history, and yet Koreans, to this day, find themselves fiercely defending the native elements of their literature, art, music, and way of life. As a result, Korean culture encompasses a wonderful collage of elements, both foreign and indigenous to the peninsula.

Literature, Art, and Religion

Korean literature draws from Chinese and Japanese roots but has its own distinctive features. Poems, romances, and short stories represent only a portion of the breadth of the Korean literary tradition. This tradition includes both folk and highly advanced literary writings and works written in Chinese as well as Korean. Before the invention of the hangul alphabet, Korean was written with Chinese characters. Although some South Koreans still use those characters, North Koreans use only hangul.

Korean poems, called *hyangga*, dating back to the 6th century, were written with Chinese characters. Hyangga were sung by Buddhist monks for religious purposes. These poems rely heavily on symbols to convey hidden meanings. For example, the hyangga *Ode to Knight Kipa* uses the image of the moon chasing

This illustration depicts a shaman dressed in traditional costume. In ancient times, shamans, usually women, were employed to drive away the evil spirits that caused illness and disease. To cure the sick, they made offerings of food and drink. In return for these offerings, the shaman, who sang, danced, and prayed, requested the spirits to leave the body of the sick person.

clouds in the sky to symbolize the speaker's attempt to read a friend's mind. Buddhist monks used the hyangga to plead for help from divine beings. A monk named Yungchon sang the *Song of the Comet* to wish away both a comet and the attacking Japanese.

Korea has a long tradition of telling and recording myths and legends. The Korean creation myth was first recorded in Chinese in the 13th century by Iryon, a great Buddhist master. The story tells of Grandpa Tangun, the first Korean king, who ascended to the throne in the 2nd millennium B.C. Tangun was born of a bear who had been transformed into a woman and of the god of wind, rain, and clouds, who had earlier chosen to descend from heaven and live among human beings. Tangun's birth supposedly took place on top of Mount Taebaek. He became the first king of Choson, made Pyongyang his capital, and reigned for 1,500 years. This myth combines native shamanistic beliefs with Chinese values.

The first literary work written in hangul was the *Songs of Flying Dragons*, a multivolume account written between 1445–47 by King Sejong's grandfather. It glorifies the creation of the Yi dynasty through a blending of myth, folklore, and historical facts. During this period, two native poetic forms became popular. Scholars began to record three-line oral poems known as *sijo*. The *kasa*—a longer narrative poetic form—also found its place in the literature of the Yi dynasty. Women writers from the upper classes wrote kasa to express the sadness and frustration they felt because of their sheltered lives.

Korean women have contributed a great deal to the literary tradition. Although women received no formal education until the 20th century, many secretly taught themselves Chinese and became talented poets. In *A Record of Sorrowful Days*, Princess Hyegyong (1735–1815) chronicles with brilliant poignancy her daily life in the royal house. She describes the traumas she endured and tragedy she witnessed when her husband, the crown prince, went mad and was eventually murdered by his own father, King Yongjo. This memoir remains both a revealing historical account of 18th-century court life in Korea and a fascinating story of a remarkable woman.

Novels began to appear in the 17th century. Among the best known are Ho Kyun's *Life of Hong Kiltong* (written in the beginning of the 17th century), Kim Man-jung's *Cloud Dream of the Nine* (written in the later 17th century), and, perhaps the most famous piece of Korean literature, *Spring Fragrance*, written anonymously in the 18th century.

Korean drama originated from harvest festivals. Masque plays, such as the *Sandae*, and puppet plays, such as the *Kkoktukaksi*, developed out of shamanistic and Buddhist rituals. During the later Yi dynasty, the *pansori* became popular. This play form involved the dramatization of tales by singers who were accompanied by drums.

Today, most fiction published in North Korea promotes the government and Kim Jong Il. Critically acclaimed writers in the country today include Yi Ki-Yong, Song Yong, and Han Sor-ya.

Chinese, Japanese, and Korean art forms have many similarities. But again, Korea has also preserved its own creative elements in the art field. Korean art is characterized by simple forms, subdued colors, humor, and natural images. Korea is known for its ceramics, especially the celadon. This highly sophisticated form of pottery was first introduced during the Koryo dynasty. Many famous murals painted on old tombs remain from the Koguryo period. Among these are the Tomb of the Wrestlers, Tomb of the Dancers, Tomb of the Hunters, and Tomb of the Four Spirits. A painting of the azure dragon of the East, the white tiger of the West, the vermilion phoenix of the South, and the tortoise of the North covers the Tomb of the Four Spirits, which is located in the province of South Pyongan.

The State Symphony Orchestra performs a composition at one of its many concerts. Orchestral music is very popular in North Korea, and much of the symphony's music is based on the revolutionary consciousness of the people, including Sea of Blood, Korea Is One, *and* Bumper Year on Chongsan Plain.

Christian missionaries founded schools and other institutions in Korea during the 19th century. The 1972 constitution allows for freedom of religion, but practice is repressed, and the 1992 constitutional revisions add that no one may use religion as a means to drag in foreign powers or disrupt the social order. Religious groups do still exist in the country. About 3 million North Koreans are Chundoists, 400,000 are Buddhists, 200,000 worship Christian faiths, and another 3 million follow some other form of traditional worship. Korea's traditional religions include Buddhism, shamanism, and Chundo Kyo, a native religion that combines elements of Buddhism and Christianity.

Children and Recreation

North Korean society places a major emphasis on the teaching of children. Not only does the government provide extensive schooling for its youth; it also has created elaborate fine arts programs for children. The Children's Cultural Palace in Pyongyang is a shining example of the focus on the young. After school, children go to the palace, where they study music, dance, foreign lan-

guages, and a variety of other artistic courses. The children also give musical and dramatic performances at the palace. Other cities in the country have smaller Children's Palaces.

Women jump seesaw at a New Year's celebration. Jumping seesaw is a common game for girls and women. Dressed in their finest clothes, women often perform somersaults while jumping. Unlike U.S. participants, who sit on the seesaw, Koreans always stand while playing the game.

Ssirum, *a martial art that is a form of wrestling, is native to Korea. It is a popular sport among farmers and fishermen and is taught in most Korean schools.*

In July 1989, an unprecedented event occurred in the city of Pyongyang. Foreigners walked the streets. Restaurants and stores supplied an abundance of goods never seen before by most North Koreans. Women wore makeup and shorter skirts. The stage was set for the Thirteenth World Festival of Youth and Students. Having missed the opportunity to cohost the 1988 Summer Olympics held in Seoul, North Korea had its turn to be in the spotlight by hosting this annual gathering of people from 180 nations. Fifteen thousand leftist youths descended upon the North Korean capital for a full week to celebrate peace, friendship, and anti-imperialism at a festival created by Eastern European youth organizations. North Koreans have now had a glimpse of how the rest of the world lives. The festival exposed the country to foreigners and their customs, and it also revealed the limitations of North Korean society to its own citizens.

Before the recent economic crisis, the North Korean government built many new theaters, libraries, museums, and vacation spots. The state supports and controls theatrical events. Mobile movie units serve rural areas with free films.

Several sports native to Korea have become popular around the world. For instance, tae kwon do, a method of self-defense that originated in Korea more than 2,000 years ago, has now become a commonly taught form of karate in the United States. It involves more sharp, quick kicking than the Japanese style of karate. In the late 1990s, about 2,000 Korean instructors were teaching tae kwon do in an estimated 120 countries. It was a demonstration sport at the 1988 and 1992 Summer Olympics.

Ssirum, which means "competition of man" in Korean, is another martial art that developed from a form of self-defense into a popular spectator sport. Based on evidence found on a Koguryo tomb, experts believe that Koreans invented this form of wrestling at least 1,500 years ago. It remains a favorite sport among Korean farmers and fishermen, and it is taught in most schools.

In recent years, North Korea has shown signs of opening its doors wider to outside cultural forces. Western influences have become more pronounced, but an ongoing fear—mostly on the government's part—of being manipulated prevents the country from changing as drastically as almost every other East Asian country has in the past decade. North Korea has a rich native culture. Unfortunately, very few people from Western countries have had the privilege of experiencing it firsthand.

During a famine relief campaign in Seoul, South Korean school children donate bags of rice that they brought from home to help North Korean children suffering from food shortages.

9

Reunification and Beyond

On January 1, 1988, President Kim Il Sung made a revolutionary declaration to his people and to the world. He stated that North and South Korea must "recognize each other's existence." On September 8, the Pyongyang newspaper, *Tong-il Shinbo* (Unification News), reported his latest words on the matter: "In order to realize unification . . . we must follow the principle of coexistence and adopt the method of leaving the two systems as they are and uniting them [under a confederation], neither side swallowing nor overwhelming the other."

This statement represented a major transformation for Kim, who, since the end of the Korean War, had denounced the idea of peaceful coexistence between the two Koreas. On July 7, 1988, South Korean president Roh Tae Woo also made history with his statement confirming that South Korea would assist North Korea in its efforts to improve relations with Japan and the United States. In the past, South Korea had always encouraged the isolation of North Korea.

At the beginning of 1989, North–South Korean relations continued to show signs of improvement. For example, the government in Pyongyang, for the first time, allowed a South Korean newspaper reporter into the country without requiring an official delegation to accompany him. But once again, all unification efforts halted on February 8, when North Korea insisted on the cancellation of the annual Team Spirit military exercises between the United States and South Korea.

These yearly military maneuvers had long been a thorn in North Korea's side. In 1990, the United States did reduce the size and scope of the exercises, but mainly for budgetary reasons. By 1993, the maneuvers resumed as usual, in response to North Korea's continuing noncooperation with officials inspecting its nuclear plants.

Meanwhile, events were progressing fast in the Communist world. In November 1989 the world watched East Germans tear down the Berlin Wall, which had divided the two Germanies since the end of World War II. This seemed to offer hope that Korea's own wall, the mass of barbed wire and mines that had long been in place at the DMZ, could itself be torn down. But Korea was not Germany, and North Korea had always set itself apart from other Communist nations. In fact, as the Communist regimes of North Korea's allies crumbled across Europe, the North Korean government tended at times to react with even greater suspicion of the outside world. Tensions especially worsened in 1992, when South Korea established diplomatic relations with the People's Republic of China, subtly alienating the north from its remaining Communist patron.

In the midst of these problems, however, North and South Korea reached another milestone in July 1990, when they signed an agreement to bring together their two prime ministers for the first time. Although North Korean prime minister Yon Hyong Muk and South Korean prime minister Kang Young Hoon were not the highest-ranking leaders of their respective countries, the decision to meet was a historic one.

In January 1990, students clap in support of President Kim Il Sung during a rally in Pyongyang. More than 50,000 students and workers attended the rally. Public adulation of the Great Leader remains strong, despite his death in 1994.

When they got together that fall, first in Seoul and then in Pyongyang, they discussed a wide range of topics: reunions of separated family members; exchanges of performers and athletes; joint business ventures; and the release of several political dissidents imprisoned in South Korea. Progress on large questions was minimal; however, the talking itself was seen as important.

Kim Il Sung's death in 1994 was another major turning point in the relationship between North and South Korea. The prime ministers and others had been on the verge of arranging a presidential-level summit. Now the mysterious Kim Jong Il was suddenly in charge in Pyongyang. Little was known about him, and even less about the extent of his control in North Korea. Some observers predicted a military overthrow of the government. Others puzzled about why he did not quickly assume the formal titles that his father had used.

Just before Kim Il Sung's death, North Korea made the startling declaration that it was no longer abiding by the 40-year-old armistice agreement, and in the spring of 1996 it briefly marched soldiers into the Joint Security Area near the DMZ. It also systematically strengthened its force at the front in the mid-1990s. None of these actions escalated, but they continued to concern the South Koreans and the United States.

In April 1996, U.S. President Clinton and South Korean President Kim Young Sam proposed a "Four Party Meeting" among North and South Korea, the United States, and China, to replace the military armistice with a document of lasting peace. North Korea responded that it wanted U.S. diplomatic recognition, more famine aid, and a lifting of remaining economic sanctions before it would agree to enter such negotiations.

The famine conditions in North Korea are now a major element in reunification negotiations. Both sides are using famine relief efforts as a way to strengthen their positions. The north demands aid as a condition for peace talks, and the south demands that aid sent to the north be labeled as gifts, to discredit Kim Jong Il.

With the spring 1997 defection of Hwang Jang Yop, a high-ranking North Korean official who largely developed the chuche ideology, the entire issue of peaceful unification has be-

Hwang Jang Yop, a high-ranking North Korean official, defected in 1997. Some people view his defection as a sign of the weakness of the North Korean government; others question the validity of Hwang Jang Yop's information.

come charged with speculation. Besides declaring that chuche and isolation had failed, Hwang also said that Kim Jong Il's government was desperate and was preparing its army for an all-out assault. Some thought that Hwang's defection represented the imminent crumbling of the government's grip on power. Others questioned how much he really knew.

In any scenario, the north and south cannot afford to fight a second installment of the Korean War, so they must find another way—negotiations, humanitarian cooperation, more trade or investment—to unite the Hermit Kingdom peacefully with the world.

GLOSSARY

Buddhism   A religion based on the life of Siddhārtha
                Gautama (the Buddha), the ancient Indian
                philosopher who taught that suffering in life is
                inherent and that one can be freed from it by
                mental and moral self-purification.

celadon   Korean pottery and porcelain ceramics first in-
                troduced during the Koryo dynasty. Today,
                Korea's celadon is internationally known for
                its superior craftsmanship.

chuche   North Korea's system of political ideas based
                on the concept of national self-reliance.

Confucianism   A philosophy based on the teachings of K'ung
                Fu-tzu (Confucius), an ancient Chinese teacher
                who stressed devotion to one's elders and jus-
                tice and peace in society.

demilitarized zone   A 2.5-mile-wide strip of neutral territory sur-
(DMZ)   rounding the 38th Parallel, which separates
                North Korea from South Korea.

dynasty   The succession of rulers from one particular
                family and the period of that family's rule.

hangul   The Korean alphabet invented in the 15th cen-
                tury.

hwarang Bands of young Korean soldiers who followed the teachings of both Buddha and Confucius during the Silla period.

hyangga Korean poems that were sung by Buddhist monks and members of the *hwarang*.

Kolpum The "bone rank" system of Silla society. Under this system, a person's background determined his or her position in society.

Korean Workers' party (KWP) The Communist political party that has supreme power in the North Korean government.

shamanism An ancient East Asian religion based on a belief in good and evil spirits.

ssirum A Korean form of wrestling that has become an internationally recognized sport.

tae kwon do A Korean form of karate that has developed from a method of self-defense into a popular sport worldwide.

Tangun The legendary founder of Korea.

38th Parallel A line of latitude on the globe that serves as the boundary between the two Koreas.

Tonghak Eastern learning; a late-19th-century religious movement that incorporated elements of traditional Korean religions and condemned government corruption.

yangban The educated upper class in Korean society that held power during the Koryo and Yi dynasties.

INDEX

PICTURE CREDITS

AP/Wide World Photos: pp. 18, 20, 78, 82, 83, 116, 121; The Bettmann Archive: pp. 51, 55, 56, 58, 60, 63; Center of the Overseas Distribution of Publications, Pyongyang, Democratic People's Republic of Korea: pp. 2, 24, 26, 27, 29, 30, 31, 47, 65–72, 85, 88, 91, 93, 95, 98, 100, 101, 103, 106, 111, 112–113, 114; Courtesy of the Freer Gallery Art, Smithsonian Institution, Washington, DC: p. 45; Reuters/Bettmann Archive: pp. 22, 119; Donna Sinisgalli: pp. 6–7; UPI/Bettmann Archive: pp. 64, 75, 84